Public Libraries and Internet Service Roles

Measuring and Maximizing Internet Services

Charles R. McClure

and

Paul T. Jaeger

American Library Association

Chicago   2009

Charles R. McClure, PhD, is the Francis Eppes Professor of Information Studies and director of the Information Use Management and Policy Institute at the School of Information Studies, Florida State University. McClure was the principal investigator on the ALA-funded project that resulted in *Planning and Role Setting for Public Libraries* (1987) and *Output Measures for Public Libraries,* 2nd ed. (1987). Since 1994, he and John Carlo Bertot have conducted the national Public Libraries and the Internet surveys, which have been funded by the Bill and Melinda Gates Foundation and the American Library Association since 2004. McClure has written extensively on topics related to the planning and evaluation of information services, federal information policy, information resources management, and digital libraries.

Paul T. Jaeger, PhD, JD, is assistant professor in the College of Information Studies and director of the Center for Information Policy and Electronic Government at the University of Maryland. His research focuses on the ways law and public policy shape access to information, with a particular focus on how law and policy affect public libraries. Jaeger is the author of more than sixty journal articles and book chapters, along with four books.

The paper used in this publication meets the minimum requirements of American National Standard for Information Sciences—Permanence of Paper for Printed Library Materials, ANSI Z39.48-1992. ∞

Library of Congress Cataloging-in-Publication Data
McClure, Charles R.
    Public libraries and Internet service roles : measuring and maximizing Internet services / Charles R. McClure and Paul T. Jaeger.
      p. cm.
    Includes bibliographical references and index.
    ISBN 978-0-8389-3576-7 (alk. paper)
    1. Libraries and the Internet—United States. 2. Internet access for library users—United States. 3. Public libraries—Aims and objectives—United States. 4. Public libraries—Social aspects—United States. 5. Libraries and society—United States. I. Jaeger, Paul T., 1974– II. Title.
    Z674.75.I58M38 2009
    025.04—dc22   2008026622

ISBN-13: 978-0-8389-3576-7

Printed in the United States of America
13 12 11 10 09   5 4 3 2 1

Contents

Preface

We have been studying the numerous relationships, questions, benefits, and challenges created by the intersection of public libraries and the Internet for a considerable amount of our careers. One of us (McClure) helped initiate the study of the impact of the Internet on public libraries fifteen years ago by establishing a national survey, Public Libraries and the Internet, which is still being conducted each year. Over that time, we have written—individually and in tandem—numerous journal articles, book chapters, and books about the Internet and public libraries and conducted numerous studies of related topics.

All of this work has demonstrated that the Internet and attendant content and services are having significant impacts on the meaning of the public library in the United States. As a result of the Internet, there have been great changes in the social roles of libraries—the ways public libraries affect their patrons and the surrounding communities—in the eyes of patrons, communities, and governments. These changes have affected the influence of public libraries in society as well as what patrons expect from libraries, what communities expect libraries to be able to do, and what duties governments place on libraries, among many other major issues.

A book like this one has become necessary to help advance both professional practice and scholarly discourse related to the social roles of public libraries. Although Internet-related changes are not necessarily altering the fundamental nature of the public library or creating issues libraries cannot handle, there can be no question at this point that the Internet is changing the roles, expectations, and effects of public libraries in society. This book is an attempt to use a wealth of historical information, statistical data, evaluation data, interview and focus group data, and policy analysis to offer a new perspective on the intersection of public library roles and the Internet.

The particular issues at hand are of enormous importance to both practitioners and researchers. Thus, this book has been written equally for library professionals, students in library and information science programs, community leaders interested in the role of public libraries, and researchers of libraries. It offers a mix of history, data, and analysis that provides new perspectives to students, researchers, professional librarians and administrators, and others. The brevity of this book reflects the intent to address major points in as pithy a manner as possible, in acknowledgment of the intense time pressures on professionals, without shortchanging the important issues being discussed. The many works cited in this book are meant to help guide those who wish to delve deeper into the literature related to these issues.

Although much has been written about the Internet in public libraries in both the academic and professional literatures, the vast majority of this discourse has taken a fairly narrow view of the issues. Too often, the literature focuses on small programs in single libraries or specific implementations or a basic cataloging of numbers of stations or types of services. Collectively, all of these mean a great deal, but individually it can be easy to lose track of their significance. The Internet may very well be the most significant event to happen to public library service in at least one hundred years, and it is essential for scholars and professionals to think about this event in societal terms.

Other information and communication technologies have certainly affected service in the modern library, from early radio and movies to television to long-playing records onward toward DVDs and CDs. The Internet is not, however, a one-way street in terms of library service. The library cannot easily select parts of the Internet, which resists any traditional notion of its use for collecting or managing information. The information is constantly changing, so it is not a static and reliable source like a book. Nor is the content necessarily correct all of the time. Further, previous technologies have not been used to place the burden of new community roles on libraries. Adding CD-ROMs to library collections in the early 1990s did not suddenly create an expectation that libraries would deliver electronic government information or ensure that citizens could have access to tax and Medicare registration forms.

Simply put, the Internet is more significant to libraries than has been any technology since the book—changing social roles, expectations, and impacts of libraries in the eyes of patrons, communities, and governments. It is essential that those who work in libraries, those who are studying to enter the profession of librarianship, and those who conduct research about libraries be able to think in terms of these major changes for libraries. The issues discussed in this book are vital to library service, planning, evaluation, research, and education. The realization of the extent to which the Internet has become ingrained in libraries is necessary for libraries to remain able to meet the needs they are expected to fulfill and not be surprised and overwhelmed by the roles and expectations that have developed for them.

Chapter 1 of the book explores the meanings of social roles and expectations of public libraries, giving particular focus to previous attempts to articulate these roles and expectations by various library researchers and professional organizations. Chapter 2 explores the historical development of these roles and expectations. Chapters 3–5 detail the roles, expectations, and impacts of public libraries in relation to the Internet on the basis of a range of data and indicators. Chapter 6 focuses on patron, community, and government expectations of public library Internet access, articulating a set of roles and expectations that attempts to reflect accurately the current reality of the social standing of public libraries. Chapter 7 details the implications of these roles and expectations for library management, planning, and evaluation. Chapter 8 examines planning for these roles and expectations in terms of community needs. Chapter 9 explores the selection of Internet-enabled roles. Chapter 10 explores the future of Internet-enabled roles in public libraries. Chapter 11 discusses these findings in light of Internet-related public policies and professional resistance to the increasing role of the Internet in public libraries. Chapter 12 explores areas for future research and topics requiring additional consideration. Chapter 13 concludes the book with contemplations about the future of the Internet and public library social roles.

Ultimately, the book has several important goals. First, it is intended to summarize a large volume of research into a manageable resource for professionals, students, and scholars. Second, it is meant to raise awareness of these important issues among professionals and offer strategies for better use of the Internet environment in the provision of library services. Third, it is written to advance scholarly discourse related to public libraries and the Internet and bring more scholarly attention to major research issues. Finally, and most important, it is an attempt to foster thinking about Internet access, services, and training in libraries from a broad social perspective.

We are strong believers that public libraries are essential to the health of democracies. It is significant that public libraries have been at the heart of battles against censorship, discrimination, abridgments of the First Amendment, McCarthyism, and the USA PATRIOT Act, among many others, over the past half century. For libraries to remain a robust and vital part of democracy, they must be fully aware of and prepared to meet the roles and expectations that patrons, communities, and governments assume they can fulfill. The Internet is now central to these roles and expectations, and we sincerely hope that this book will help libraries, library professionals, students, and researchers to ensure that patrons, communities, and governments can continue to rely on public libraries in the future.

1

Identifying Social and Service Roles and Expectations for Public Libraries

In the United States, public libraries are institutions which, since their inception, have played specific roles and met certain expectations within society. As a review of historical documents, professional positions, and scholarly research demonstrates, public libraries generally have moved from the early social roles as providers of prescriptive information about morals and behavior to modern social roles as a marketplace of ideas that provides a diverse array of materials on many topics from multiple perspectives.

Public librarians, since the mid-1990s, enthusiastically embraced the Internet and are leaders in providing public Internet access and services, with nearly 100% of libraries being connected to the Internet by 2007. In that time, Internet access and related services have accelerated from a novel new way to look for information to an essential part of many services libraries provide and a key part of what users, communities, and governments expect from libraries. Most traditional library services, from reference to cataloging, are now entirely dependent on networked computers. More significant, the provision of Internet access and training has made libraries a central part of many new activities that support society, such as e-government access and emergency services.

Jesse Shera (1976) wrote that the development of the library should be viewed in light of both the evolution of the contents and services of the library and the relationship between the library and society. This book examines the development of social and service roles of and related expectations for public libraries in light of the evolving Internet and networked environment and how that environment may have affected the development of the roles of public libraries in society. In spite of these clear Internet-inspired changes, some in the library community, both professionals and researchers, downplay the importance of the Internet to librarianship or view it as a threat to the traditional social positions of public libraries. Nonetheless, not only are Internet-enabled roles and expectations inextricably linked to public libraries, the capacities of the Internet have simultaneously reinforced the traditional social positions and expanded the ways libraries can serve their patrons and communities.

By drawing on data from 1994 to 2007 related to the provision of Internet access and services in public libraries, in this book we explore the decisions made by public libraries regarding the provision of Internet services and the groups and contexts to which these services are targeted in relation to the contemporary social roles of and the related social expectations for public libraries of patrons, communities, and governments. We argue that public libraries have yet to reconcile traditional social roles and expectations effectively with their efforts to serve as community provider of Internet access and a range of network services.

BASIC CONCEPTS AND TERMS

The social roles of public libraries can be understood as the ways public libraries affect, intentionally or otherwise, their patrons and surrounding communities. These social roles have evolved significantly over the past two centuries, particularly in the United States. In many ways, the evolution of the public library in the United States can be seen as an evolution of its social roles. Research related to public libraries in contemporary society has identified different ways the social roles of public libraries can be viewed.

In this book we also specifically examine the social roles of public libraries in terms of the service roles through which public libraries try to affect their patrons and their communities. The emphasis on providing Internet access and services has influenced the social roles public libraries are trying to fulfill and may be reshaping these roles quite substantially. Service roles have also radically altered patron, community, and government expectations for public libraries. A key theme of this book is that public libraries in the United States have yet to integrate fully the evolving Internet-enabled service roles into the traditional public library service roles.

To clarify terms, we refer to public library *social roles* as large societal purposes for which libraries exist and which communities, individuals, and governments expect as the public library's contributions to society, whereas *service roles* are specific attempts by libraries to respond to social roles and meet these expectations through traditional and Internet-enabled services (see figure 1 later in this chapter). As such, service roles are aspects of larger social roles. Service roles are a primary means by which libraries operationalize and implement social roles to achieve professional goals and fulfill expectations for the library.

Although we generally use *service roles* throughout this book, there are some variations on the term. The term *service roles* was first used in the 1987 Public Library Association (PLA) book (McClure et al. 1987). In the later PLA books described below, *service responses* was the term used. When discussing the ideas from these books, we generally employ the respective versions of the term. Overall, in considering the ideas proposed in the present book, it may be most useful to think in terms of *Internet-enabled service roles and responses,* which is more comprehensive and better reflects the realities of contemporary library service.

Traditional service roles and responses are public library activities that have been endorsed by PLA since 1987 and provide a road map for the activities libraries are to provide and how they are to meet community and societal expectations. The discussion in this book differentiates between *traditional* public library service roles—which have been published by the PLA in 1987, 2001, and 2007—and *Internet-enabled* service roles—which we identify and discuss at length in this book. In 1987, under the direction of the PLA, researchers worked to identify specific, quantifiable service roles for public libraries. These have been updated and revised in 2001 and 2007. Although public libraries have clearly had social roles since their inception, the focus of this book is the transition from traditional service roles to Internet-enabled service roles over the past several decades.

Figure 1 illustrates a relatively complex set of concepts and relationships and indicates those aspects addressed in this book. Point 1 on the figure suggests that there are societal needs of public libraries, that is, purposes, roles, and services that are *needed* by society. These needs are largely determined by the public library community. Point 2 recognizes, however, that there are also societal *expectations* of public libraries, that is, what members of society expect or believe are appropriate purposes, roles, and services. Societal needs of and societal expectations for public libraries may or may not be the same. If they are not the same, then there is a disconnect between what the library community thinks society needs and what society expects of public libraries.

These needs and expectations form a set of public library social roles, as demonstrated at point 3. The degree to which these social roles are agreed upon or even identified as appropriate for the public library community may be problematic. As part of these social roles, public librarians have constructed service roles and responses, which are intended to meet the needs and expectations of society. These service roles and responses can be further differentiated into traditional service roles and responses (those described by PLA) and Internet-enabled service roles and responses (which are discussed in greater detail later in this book). The public library service roles and responses are depicted within a dotted rectangle since they may be difficult to differentiate from the larger public library social roles. The service roles and responses can be conscious efforts on the part of librarians in formal or informal planning efforts or they may be provided without a conscious plan. But all libraries provide service roles and responses, regardless of whether they are part of a formal planning process.

At points 4 and 5, the success of the provision of the public library service roles and responses is affected by local, state, and federal factors. The library has more control of or influence on local factors than it does on factors at the state and federal level; nonetheless, both sets of factors affect point 6, the impacts and benefits of library services on both society and individual library users. The

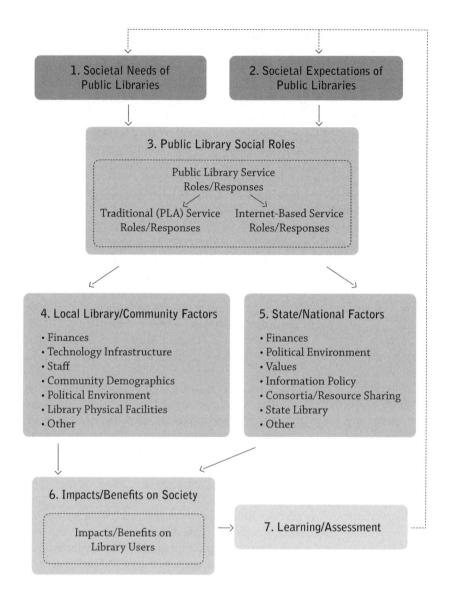

Figure 1 Basic concepts and relationships

situational factors noted in points 4 and 5 are discussed only in passing in this book, but it is important to recognize their presence.

At point 6, the public library community has developed numerous approaches to measure the impacts and benefits of implementing public library service roles and responses (e.g., Bertot and Davis 2004; Matthews 2007; McClure 2008). The impacts to and benefits for library users are included within a dotted rectangle within the broader range of impacts to and benefits on society since measures for each may be related. The extent to which public libraries do, in fact, engage in formal assessment of the effect of library services on society and library users varies considerably from library to library.

Once (or perhaps if) the impacts and benefits can be determined from public library service roles and responses (whether they have been consciously selected or not), some type of learning or assessment informs the perceptions of members of society about the degree to which their expectations of the public library were, in fact, met. Simultaneously, learning and assessment should be applied to the accuracy of public librarian's perceptions of the social needs of patrons, communities, and governments. Clearly there are likely to be numerous other factors related to public library social roles and their development and use in society—but the depiction in figure 1 provides a framework for discussing social roles and library planning.

Early on, public library social roles reflected the concept of the library as arbiter of morals and guide to social conformity. A significant shift in these social roles in the early to mid-twentieth century led public libraries to become a place of the free access, exchange, and expression of diverse ideas. Now, the provision of Internet access has become an essential element affecting the established social roles of public libraries. In this rapidly changing information society, it is vital to "examine libraries from a broader social context in order to better understand the complex roles that libraries play in their communities" (Burke and Martin 2004, 405). This book examines the choices public libraries are currently making as providers of Internet access and services in relation to the traditional social roles of public libraries along with the social expectations related to these choices. In this book, Internet-enabled services should be seen as being inclusive of the elements necessary to provide Internet access to patrons—computers and related hardware, Internet connectivity, Internet-enabled resources, licensed products and databases, digital collections, and related resources.

DESCRIBING SOCIAL ROLES OF PUBLIC LIBRARIES

Overall, the perceived social roles of public libraries are usually "summarized as information, education, recreation, culture, and economic regeneration" (Williamson 2000, 179), paralleling what are often identified as the objectives of modern public libraries (Hafner 1987). A more insightful way to generalize the social roles of public libraries may be as the provider of free access to information to all patrons, operated as publicly funded yet independent organizations to the benefit of the community and staffed with educated professionals who provide unprejudiced expert advice as a public service (Webster 1995).

The social roles of public libraries have also been examined directly in terms of their impacts and the benefits and values they provide (Debono 2002). Generally, these discussions focus on the public library as providing an educational impact through the materials and resources available, an economic impact through meeting the information needs of local business and employment seekers and through potentially fostering of local development, and a community impact through promoting culture, diversity, and involvement in meetings, organizations, and political activities (Kerslake and Kinnell 1998). Examining the social roles of public libraries in terms of benefits, values, and impacts is usually intended to justify resources, improve services, document demographic changes, or provide information to decision makers (Debono 2002).

Building on studies related to social impacts, some recent scholarship has focused on the social roles of public libraries in terms of the promotion of social capital. Social capital encompasses the tangible and intangible ways an organization enhances the social functions of the surrounding community (Putnam 1999). Public libraries can be viewed in terms of adding social capital to communities through facilitating community meetings, cultural programs, social venues, and local partnerships (Bourke 2005). Libraries "build social capital by providing a shared, public space for a variety of different groups within the community, accommodating diverse needs and enhancing social interaction and trust" (Hillenbrand 2005, 8). Little literature outside of library and information science (LIS) studies, however, examines or even acknowledges the role of public libraries in building social capital in communities.

Regardless of one's perspective on the social roles of the library, that the public library has myriad social roles is beyond question. In fact, public libraries are one of the few remaining public places that have developed and recognized social roles. Whereas many traditional public spaces in communities—the town square, the public gardens, the community market, and other places that serve to foster interaction among community members—have become less visible or ceased to exist, the public library continues to be an extremely important public space (Given and Leckie 2003; Leckie and Hopkins 2002). There are likely to be differences between the social roles of public libraries in different communities. In some places, the public library "is the jewel of the community"; in others it may not be valued by the community (Hafner 1987, 108). Nearly 90% of Americans do, however, believe public libraries to be as valuable or more valuable than other tax-supported public services and accord libraries a high level of trust (*Economist* 1998). Thus, in most locales, the public library remains a prominent "public space in which individuals may engage in a range of social and informational activities" (Given and Leckie 2003, 365).

In 1987 a research team developed a formalized study of the service roles of public libraries at the behest of the PLA and the American Library Association (ALA). The results of this effort, *Planning and Role Setting for Public Libraries*, asserted that public libraries have established eight specific roles in communities: activity center, information center, education support center, independent learning center, popular materials access, childhood learning center, reference materials and support, and research center (McClure et al. 1987).

The notion of public library service roles, when first published in 1987, was a concept explained as

> profiles of library service emphases. Taken as a group, they provide a catalog of
> library service images. Each [of the eight] roles is a shorthand way of describ-
> ing a combination of factors important in planning: What the library is trying
> to do, Who the library is trying to serve, and What resources the library needs
> to achieve these ends (McClure et al. 1987, 28).

Over the years, the notion of service roles and later service responses for public libraries has been revised, updated, and modified.

As table 1 demonstrates, each of these eight service roles has specific impacts on the community and patrons of the library. Each role is based on direct social involvement in the community and has clear implications for library planning, management, resources, and advocacy, serving as the nexus of the library's relationship with the community.

Table 1   Eight Key Service Roles of Public Libraries

Library Service Role	Examples	Key Community Benefits
Community Activities Center	• Discussion groups • Issues forums • Lectures • Exhibits and performances • Health testing • Voter registration	• Increased discussion and awareness of issues • Availability of social services • Central location for community events • Community communication network
Community Information Center	• Clearinghouse for information on organizations, events, issues, and services • Contact lists • Job information • Referral networks • Information fairs	• Single source for community information • Improved self-sufficiency for community members • Link of needs to providers and resources • Assistance for community decision making
Formal Education Support Center	• Educational materials and assistance for students • Library tours • Instruction using library resources • Homework assistance • Coordination with local schools	• Resources and services for students in elementary schools, secondary schools, community colleges, technical schools, colleges and universities, training programs, and adult and continuing education programs • Study location • Supplement to resources in school and academic libraries
Independent Learning Center	• Educational materials and assistance for learning independent of formalized educational settings • Occupational counseling and skills assessments • Support for cultural and personal interests	• Self-determined and self-paced learning resources • Materials and services for self-improvement • Increased knowledge about community, social, and political issues

(cont.)

Table 1 Eight Key Social Roles of Public Libraries (cont.)

Library Service Role	Examples	Key Community Benefits
Popular Materials Library	• High interest and popular materials in various formats for various age groups	• Availability of wide variety of high demand materials for reading, listening, and viewing • Supplement to materials available in local bookstores and other outlets
Preschoolers' Door to Learning	• Materials to help parents promote reading skills • Storytelling and children's story hour • Outreach to daycare programs	• Trained staff members help children and parents promote reading and learning • Resources for parents • Children prepared to start school
Reference Library	• Reference materials related to professional and personal interests • Specialized research services • Consumer information • Cooperative services	• Convenient access to timely information needed for daily decision making in professional and personal contexts • Critical information for local government • Critical information for local business
Research Center	• In-depth, specific, and detailed materials on research topics • Subject materials for particular types of professional research (i.e., legal, medical) • Scholarly research materials	• Materials for professional research • Materials for scholarly research • Enhanced status of community as intellectual hub

Source: McClure et al. (1987).

Immediately after the publication of *Planning and Role Setting for Public Libraries* in 1987, there was considerable interest in using these roles in planning and advocacy. The PLA's publicity campaign to promote these library service roles was significant, with many libraries publicly displaying their roles. The manual that originally detailed these roles has sold nearly 20,000 copies, primarily in the first ten years after its publication. By the mid- to late 1990s, use of and advocacy based on these roles dramatically fell as public libraries became interested in other services, especially libraries that were Internet enabled.

The focus on the Internet and network-based technologies changed many aspects of library service roles and the planning and management of public libraries, as libraries moved from thinking about social roles, library service roles, and activism in the community to providing networked technologies and services. Indeed, the publication of an expanded version of the planning manual in 1999 (more than 7,700 copies sold) and a streamlined version of the 1999 book in 2001 (more than 6,500 copies sold) did not provoke the same interest in public library service roles in the public library community (Himmel and Willson 1999; Nelson 2001). The focus on and perceived importance of public library Internet access and services seemingly began to overshadow many of the service roles in which the library was previously engaged. Six years after the publication of the initial service roles, McClure noted:

> While the notion of service roles is a good one, and one that helps librarians better think about what services are most important for a particular community, these roles need to be more locally developed. The existing ones are too traditional, somewhat out of date, and fail to include a range of service roles that are technologically oriented, e.g., the "Electronic Networked Library." (1993, 199)

This recommendation was based on several public library research efforts conducted by McClure at the time. Researchers and practitioners recognized the need to consider Internet-enabled service roles in the early 1990s, but it was unclear if they might present an enhancement of established social roles or an alteration of established social roles.

The PLA introduced the 2001 version of library service roles, now referred to as service responses; interestingly, none of the roles was directly related to the Internet or Internet services (see figure 2). The 2001 manual explained the service responses as follows:

> What exactly is a service response? How does a service response differ from the eight library roles introduced in *Planning and Role Setting for Public Libraries* in 1987? In simple terms, *a service response is what a library does for or offers to the public in an effort to meet a set of well-defined community needs.* Roles are broadly defined categories of service; they describe what the library does in a very general way. Service responses, on the other hand, are very distinct ways that libraries serve the public. They represent the gathering and deployment of specific critical resources to produce a specific public benefit or result (Nelson 2001, 146).

In fact, the intent of the original eight service roles was similar to, if not the same as, the social responses that were developed in 2001. Both respond to identified community needs; both suggest specific types of services to be provided; and both offer a means by which ongoing evaluation can be conducted to determine the degree to which the service roles are, in fact, being accomplished.

To a large extent the 2001 responses were a refinement of the 1987 roles, adding more detail and a wider assortment of possible roles. But the most interesting aspect of the 2001 library service responses was the lack of any mention of roles related to community needs for Internet-enabled services. Indeed, the index in the 2001 manual lists only two instances of the words "Internet" or "world wide web." As shown in figure 2, the 2001 service responses maintained

Basic Literacy. A library that offers Basic Literacy service addresses the need to read and to perform other essential daily tasks.

Business and Career Information. A library that offers Business and Career Information service addresses a need for information related to business, careers, work, entrepreneurship, personal finances, and obtaining employment.

Commons. A library that provides a Commons environment helps address the need of people to meet and interact with others in their community and to participte in public discourse about community issues.

Community Referral. A library that offers Community Referral addresses the need for information related to services provided by community agencies and organizations.

Consumer Information. A library that provides Consumer Information service helps to satisfy the need for information to make informed consumer decisions and to help residents become more self-sufficient.

Cultural Awareness. A library that offers Cultural Awareness service helps satisfy the desire of community residents to gain an understanding of their own cultural heritage and the cultural heritage of others.

Current Topics and Titles. A library that provides Current Topics and Titles helps to fulfill community residents' appetite for information about popular culture and social trends and their desire for satisfying recreational experiences.

Formal Learning Support. A library that offers Formal Learning Support helps students who are enrolled in a formal program of education or who are pursuing their education through a program of homeschooling to attain their educational goals.

General Information. A library that offers General Information helps meet the need for information and answers to questions on a broad array of topics related to work, school, and personal life.

Government Information. The library that offers Government Information service helps satisfy the need for information about elected officials and government agencies that enables people to participate in the democratic process.

Information Literacy. A library that provides Information Literacy service helps address the need for skills related to finding, evaluating, and using information effectively.

Lifelong Learning. A library that provides Lifelong Learning service helps address the desire for self-directed personal growth and development opportunities.

Local History and Genealogy. A library that offers Local History and Genealogy service addresses the desire of community residents to know and better understand personal or community heritage.

Figure 2   Library service responses, 2001

Source: Nelson (2001, 65).

a traditional view of public library service roles and the manner in which these roles meet the expectations of the local community.

As Internet use by the public has increased since 1994, so too has public library Internet connectivity, jumping from 20.9% in 1994 to 99.1% in 2007 (McClure, Bertot, and Zweizig 1994; McClure, Jaeger, and Bertot 2007). Also during the late 1990s and early 2000s, the Bill and Melinda Gates Foundation launched a large-scale initiative that provided public libraries with workstations, networking technologies, and technology training. It is unclear, however, if public librarians carefully thought through this influx of technology and training in light of traditional service roles. This focus on the Internet and the networked environment has seemingly led libraries to view their priorities more and more in terms of providing Internet access and technology use rather than in pursing or rethinking the traditional social roles or those that were identified in 1987, expanded in 1999 and 2001, and updated again in 2007.

The 2007 service responses identified by the PLA only minimally account for the new Internet-enabled roles of the public library, although many of the 2007 roles are discussed as Internet dependent (see figure 3). Connecting to the online world, in fact, is identified as a single role, in spite of the fact that many of the other roles can be at least partially fulfilled through the use of

Be an Informed Citizen: Local, National, and World Affairs. Residents will have the information they need to support and promote democracy, to fulfill their civic responsibilities at the local, state, and national levels, and to fully participate in community decision making.

Build Successful Enterprises: Business and Nonprofit Support. Business owners and nonprofit organization directors and their managers will have the resources they need to develop and maintain strong viable organizations.

Celebrate Diversity: Cultural Awareness. Residents will have programs and services that promote appreciation and understanding of their personal heritage and the heritage of others in the community.

Connect to the Online World: Public Internet Access. Residents will have high-speed access to the digital world with no unnecessary restrictions or fees to ensure that everyone can take advantage of the ever-growing resources and services available through the Internet.

Create Young Readers: Early Literacy. Children from birth to five will have programs and services designed to ensure that they will enter school ready to learn to read, write, and listen.

Discover Your Roots: Genealogy and Local History. Residents and visitors will have the resources they need to connect the past with the present through their family histories and to understand the history and traditions of the community.

Figure 3   Library service responses, 2007

Source: Nelson (2008, 47).

Express Creativity: Create and Share Content. Residents will have the services and support they need to express themselves by creating original print, video, audio, or visual content in a real-world or online environment.

Get Facts Fast: Ready Reference. Residents will have someone to answer their questions on a wide array of topics of personal interest.

Know Your Community: Community Resources and Services. Residents will have a central source for information about the wide variety of programs, services, and activities provided by community agencies and organizations.

Learn to Read and Write: Adult, Teens, and Family Literacy. Adults and teens will have the support they need to improve their literacy skills in order to meet their personal goals and fulfill their responsibilities as parents, citizens, and workers.

Make Career Choices: Job and Career Development. Adults and teens will have the skills and resources they need to identify career opportunities that suit their individual strengths and interests.

Make Informed Decisions: Health, Wealth, and Other Life Choices. Residents will have the resources they need to identify and analyze risks, benefits, and alternatives before making decisions that affect their lives.

Satisfy Curiosity: Lifelong Learning. Residents will have the resources they need to explore topics of personal interest and continue to learn throughout their lives.

Stimulate Imagination: Reading, Viewing, and Listening for Pleasure. Residents who want materials to enhance their leisure time will find what they want when and where they want them and will have the help they need to make choices from among the options.

Succeed in School: Homework Help. Students will have the resources they need to succeed in school.

Understand How to Find, Evaluate, and Use Information: Information Fluency. Residents will know when they need information to resolve an issue or answer a question and will have the skills to search for, locate, evaluate, and effectively use information to meet their needs.

Visit a Comfortable Place: Physical and Virtual Spaces. Residents will have safe and welcoming physical places to meet and interact with others or to sit quietly and read and will have open and accessible virtual spaces that support networking.

Welcome to the United States: Service for New Immigrants. New immigrants and refugees will have information on citizenship, English Language Learning, employment, public schooling, health and safety, available social services, and any other topics that they need to participate successfully in American life.

Figure 3 Library service responses, 2007 (cont.)

the Internet and related technologies. Perhaps more surprising is the fact that the 2007 publication does not account for new roles that have developed, even though libraries have provided a wider array of social benefits via technology and communities have greater expectations for Internet-enabled information and services in libraries, as is detailed later.

The new definition of service responses is largely the same as that offered in 2001. The 2007 version, however notes the following:

> They [the service responses] are, however, designed to describe the most common clusters of services and programs that libraries provide. . . . The descriptions and examples offered are provided to help library planners see the many possibilities that exist for matching their services to the unique needs of their communities (Garcia and Nelson 2007, 2).

The 1987, 2001, and 2007 roles show a remarkable similarity in terms of their general thrust and only a limited effort to recognize Internet/Web/digital information and other electronic services as a means to meet community needs. In short, the 2007 roles—aside from including accessing the Internet—seem to show little recognition of the enormous technological changes of the past two decades and have limited relevance to Internet-enabled services documented in various studies conducted since 1994.

The differences between the 2007 roles and those articulated in 1987 are nevertheless interesting. The 1987 library service roles focus on larger concepts; the 2007 roles have been narrowed down to specific activities, such as genealogy research. A further major shift is detailing the types of resources, partners, audiences, and policy implications embedded in the roles. The 1987 roles were tied directly to large-scale community benefits; the 2007 roles are tied to program impacts. But our overriding conclusion is that the PLA service roles have *not* changed much in twenty years, and Internet access and services in public libraries apparently have had little impact on the development of these 2007 roles.

Social roles and community expectations for public libraries are now strongly, perhaps inextricably, tied to the provision of Internet access, assistance, and a range of services and applications. Minimizing the realities of the impact of the Internet on public libraries' service roles, as the 2007 PLA list of roles does, indicates insufficient recognition of the significant move away from some traditional service roles and the modification of other roles as a result of the Internet.

The rise of the Internet in society was a rapid, groundbreaking technological change that may have enhanced or even altered the primary social roles public libraries have developed over the course of nearly two hundred years. The speed with which Internet-based access and services have come to limit librarians' attention to the more traditional social roles of public libraries certainly merits serious consideration, particularly within the context of the historical development of the social roles of public libraries.

The major changes in information technology and individual, community, and government use of technology since the mid-1990s have resulted in shifting social roles of and social expectations for public libraries. These changes may also be causing alterations in the profession's view of itself. The ubiquity of the Internet makes it a significantly unique influence on public libraries. Previous information technology evolutions over the past century have provided new means for the delivery of information; the Internet provided a huge increase in the amount of information, new types of services, and new ways that information can be used and linked.

In addition, the Internet serves as a means to increase communication channels and build social interconnectivity. Instead of being a one-way information flow, the Internet features many types of multidirectional interactions and information exchanges, from basic applications such as e-mail to cutting-edge Web 2.0 technologies (Stephens 2007). The range of unique applications from the Internet means that it has, and will continue to have, very different impacts on public library service roles and societal expectations of public libraries than did previous technological advances such as video cassettes, compact discs, or microfilm.

2

The Development of the
Social Roles of Public Libraries

For many years, the public library has had a unique, socially significant position in American society. From the beginning of the republic, some leaders saw the public library as a social institution that could simultaneously diffuse knowledge to the citizenry and prevent the wealthy and socially elite from having hegemonic domination over learning and education. Benjamin Franklin was the first prominent political leader to advocate the development of libraries to provide political and educational resources to citizens (Gray 1993; Harris 1976). By the 1810s, libraries had become official repositories for many national and state government publications, eventually leading to the creation of the Federal Depository Library program to make available at specified libraries copies of all government publications (Morehead 1999).

Franklin's belief that the public library should have the primary function of promoting equality and raising the quality of national discourse was, however, somewhat unusual in his generation (Augst 2001). Well into the twentieth century, many more civic and political leaders believed that public libraries could provide a civilizing influence on the masses and be a means to shape the populace into adhering to social expectations (Augst 2001; Harris 1973, 1976). Libraries were "supported more or less as alternatives to taverns and streets," and librarians "viewed themselves as arbiters of morality" (Jones 1993, 135). The objective of public librarians was often expressed in "broadly religious terms," as if it were a mission to save the lost masses (Garrison 1993, 37). This elitist attitude was reflected in public library selections of materials for the public betterment and attempts to be social stewards of the general population (Augst 2001; Harris 1976; Heckart 1991; Morehead 1999; Wiegand 1976, 1996).

This first primary set of social roles embraced by public libraries was unwaveringly prescriptive. The "felt cultural superiority of librarians led them to a concept of the library as a sort of benevolent school of social ethics" (Garrison 1993, 40). Andrew Carnegie's philanthropic library building activities between 1886 and 1917 further enhanced this social role by making public libraries a means for improving the corporate skills of members of the public (Garrison 1993; Van Slyck 1995). During the period of prescriptive social roles for public libraries, leaders of the library profession were greatly opposed to social change and feared the labor rights movement and other forces reshaping American society. Library leaders even generally felt that the growth of newspapers was a threat to the prescribed social order, of which public libraries considered themselves an important part (Garrison 1993; McCrossen 2006; Preer 2006).

By the 1930s, however, public libraries began to turn away from trying to act as means of social control. It took the rise of fascism and a world war, but ultimately public libraries created and adopted a new primary social role as the veritable marketplace of ideas, offering materials that represented a diversity of views and opposing censorship and other social controls (Gellar 1974; Heckart 1991). Many libraries had begun to take on a social service mission by the early 1930s, appearing earliest in public libraries in urban settings and those with largely immigrant patron populations (Fiske 1959). This dramatic change in social roles "emerged in an environment in which the concept of the public library's social responsibility was itself changing radically" (Gellar 1974, 1367).

Numerous factors affected this reorientation of the social roles of public libraries. But the key change was the effect fascist governments were having on public access to information in many parts of the world in the late 1930s, specifically through lethal suppression of expression, closing of libraries, and public book burnings (Gellar 1984; Robbin 1996; Stielow 2001). In reaction to these global events, the ALA passed its Library Bill of Rights in 1939 and began the swing toward the modern ideal of the public library as society's marketplace of ideas (Berninghausen 1953; Gellar 1984; Robbin 1996).

A central component of this new stance was the unswerving assertion that voters must have access to a full range of perspectives on all significant political and social issues (Samek 2001). One writer, in 1953, pithily explained the need for libraries to hold to this then-new stance of providing diverse information from numerous perspectives because "a democratic society has need for all the information it can get" (Berninghausen 1953, 813). This commitment to diversity of perspectives and to battling censorship was reinforced in society when public libraries actively resisted government intrusions into library collections and patron reading habits, particularly during the McCarthy era (Jaeger and Burnett 2005). Though various censorship efforts have continued to affect public libraries since the McCarthy era, such as the FBI's infamous Library Awareness Program in the 1980s, the public library has become identified in society as a marketplace of ideas that is open to all and as a defender of public access to information (Foerstel 1991, 2004; Jaeger and Burnett 2005).

The invention of many home-use entertainment technologies led libraries to begin to include new types of media—videocassettes, CDs, DVDs—in the mission to offer users a diversity of materials with many perspectives (Pittman 2001). As the Internet swiftly gained social prominence and significance in the 1990s, public libraries began to add Internet access and a range of new services through numerous media that enabled patrons to gain access to a wide expanse of information and ideas. Many assertions have been made that the provision of Internet access and these services in libraries can serve as a natural extension of the established social roles of libraries. By providing a new avenue by which to access information and by providing access to many materials the library could not otherwise provide for reasons of cost, space, or scarcity, the Internet can be considered a robust source of diverse, and often otherwise unavailable, information for patrons (Bennett 2001; Kranich 2001).

The development of the public library through the nineteenth and twentieth centuries solidified the library's social position so that, at the beginning of the twenty-first century, the public library stands as a primary source of information that is equally available to all citizens and residents. This provision of information has created certain social roles for public libraries in the United States. Simply put, as the nation has matured, the social role of the public library has matured from a repository of texts to a marketplace of ideas (Heckart 1991). There now exists an expectation that the public library will provide equal access to a wide range of information and views in numerous formats, often in a variety of languages representing a diverse array of perspectives on social and political issues (Jaeger and Burnett 2005). For people with limited or no other access to published and electronic materials, the expected social function of public libraries is to ensure access to newspapers and periodicals, books of nonfiction and fiction, the Internet, music, movies, and more. For all people, the public library is now seen as a social and virtual space where all ages and walks of life can mix, exchange views, access materials, and engage in public discourse (Goulding 2004; Jaeger and Burnett 2005).

The eight established service roles of libraries identified in 1987 are manifestations of the goals of the marketplace of ideas. As detailed in table 1, these roles foster community discussion and participation, educate citizens of all ages, enhance the political process, and create forums for public expression of diverse ideas and perspectives. They are not only an outgrowth of the concept of the marketplace of ideas; they also serve to reinforce the importance of the marketplace of ideas to the community and patrons.

In 1993, McClure, Ryan, and Moen proposed, on the basis of a study funded by OCLC, several "new" roles that could be promoted by public libraries in the networked environment (32):

- traditional safety net in preserving access to all
- electronic navigator and intermediary
- provider of electronic information to remote users
- coordinator of local community electronic information resources
- switching station for electronic information resources and services

All of these potential service roles, however, would encourage the broad social role of the public library as the marketplace of ideas and information.

This position as the marketplace of ideas would seem to be enhanced ineluctably by the growth of Internet usage. The Internet is, in many ways, akin to a marketplace of ideas, where a dialogue on myriad topics is generated in cyberspace between users on the basis of their information needs and personal interests. As a result, Internet access and services are now becoming an essential part of public libraries and the services they provide. As of 2007, 99.7% of public libraries in the United States had Internet access and 99.1% of those libraries provided public access to the Internet (McClure, Jaeger, and Bertot 2007). For most patrons, walking into a library and finding no public Internet access would be as unexpected, and as unacceptable, as walking into a library and finding no printed materials. This free Internet access has created new ways to reach many specific user populations, from children (Druin 2005) to older adults (Xie and Jaeger, forthcoming). Accordingly, the social roles of public libraries now include being a provider of Internet access—computers, connectivity, training, and Internet-enabled services and materials.

Some might suggest that certain aspects of the Internet and related technologies run contrary to or undermine the established social roles of public libraries as a marketplace of ideas. New technologies can be expensive, and in many libraries the costs of these new technologies are cutting into spending on more traditional and permanent materials; at the same time, much of the information provided by the Internet—particularly commercial information—falls outside the parameters of information provided by other media in the library (Brown and Duguid 2002; Buschman 2003). And though some of these concerns are not without basis, clearly none of these potential drawbacks means that the Internet does not have an important place in the library—particularly since the cost of technology tends to go down as it becomes more commonplace. But can even well-planned implementation of the Internet in libraries also prove detrimental to other services?

The issues discussed above point to the conclusion that the provision of Internet access and service is reshaping the social roles of public libraries and the expectations of library patrons, communities, and even governments. The impacts of the provision of Internet access on the social roles of public libraries can be analyzed both to provide libraries with a better understanding of the present situation and to facilitate planning and decision making related to Internet access. Does the provision of Internet access and services in libraries ultimately serve as a new resource for the marketplace of ideas—or as the beginning of a shift away from the marketplace of ideas? In either case, it seems quite possible that the provision of Internet access and related technologies will significantly change—by enhancing or by altering—the social roles of public libraries in society.

For example, one might argue that in the late 1990s the social role of public libraries as a marketplace of ideas was augmented by the social role as a safety net for accessing Internet services (McClure 1993). From its initial appearance, the Internet has resulted in a "digital divide" in which, because of geography, income level, ethnic type, educational attainment, and other factors, some residents are unable to access Internet services—except through the public library (Horrigan 2007). To serve its role as a marketplace of ideas, public libraries became guarantors of public access to Internet service to all. The degree to which this was a conscious decision on the part of the public library community is unclear, but many national leaders and policymakers found that this social role of public libraries did, in fact, meet important societal needs of inclusiveness.

In society at large, public libraries are often perceived by patrons as a place of "communal ownership and use of information" (Bennett 2001, 257). Still, the decisions made by public librarians in terms of the services they provide can affect and shape the social roles of libraries. Libraries "are intricately intertwined with the greater social patterns of society as a whole and of the communities in which they are situated" (Burke and Martin 2004, 422). The types of services they provide, the groups at whom these services are aimed, those who are encouraged to participate in certain library activities, the materials that are made available, and numerous other decisions affect who visits a public library and what is expected of the library when they arrive. The rise of the Internet in society and within the library appears to have greatly affected the social roles of public libraries since the mid-1990s, with a significant increase in the impacts as the Internet has become more widely established in libraries and patrons, communities, and governments have discovered all the societal benefits that such Internet access provides.

3

Internet Access in Social Roles of Public Libraries

Key indicators of the attention accorded to providing public library Internet access come from national surveys conducted since 1994. This chapter and the next two examine different aspects of how the Internet is becoming intertwined with the social roles of public libraries. This chapter looks at the Internet as a part of providing access. Chapter 4 examines the roles related to Internet training and services, and Chapter 5 explores the policy-based Internet roles of libraries.

The most recent data in this book are drawn from study results recorded in *Public Libraries and the Internet 2007* (Bertot et al. 2007). The 2007 survey continues the research of previous surveys conducted by John Carlo Bertot and Charles R. McClure since 1994 but expands the scope of the areas studied (for more information on previous studies, see www.ii.fsu.edu).

The 2007 survey was part of a larger study funded by the ALA to gain a better understanding of public library technology access and funding, which included the national survey, case site visits to public libraries in selected states, and a survey of state librarians. The overall study's primary focus was to obtain comprehensive data related to these topics and explore the issues public libraries encounter when planning for, implementing, and operating their public-access technology components (e.g., workstations, bandwidth, services, and resources).

The 2007 *Public Libraries and the Internet* study employed a web-based survey approach to gather data, with a mailed survey participation invitation letter from the ALA sent to the directors of libraries in the sample. The letter introduced the study, provided information regarding the study sponsors and research team, explained the study purpose and goals, provided instructions on how to access and complete the electronic survey, and gave contact information for any questions participants might have.

As with previous studies, the 2007 study obtained data that enabled analysis by the following categories: Metropolitan status (e.g., urban, suburban, and rural), which was determined from official designations employed by the Census Bureau, the Office of Management and Budget, and other government agencies; Poverty (less than 20% [low], 20–40% [medium], and greater than 40% [high]); State (the fifty states plus the District of Columbia); and National. Given the quality of the data, findings could be generalized to each of these four categories. Finally, the survey explored topics that pertain to both public library system and outlet (branch) level data, requiring a complex sample.

The study team used the 2002 public library dataset available from the National Center for Education Statistics (NCES), the most recent file at the time the geocoding process began, as a sample frame. The team employed the services of the GeoLib database (www.geolib.org/PLGDB.cfm) to geocode the NCES public library universe file in order to calculate the poverty rates for public library outlets. Given the time frame of the study, GeoLib was able to geocode 16,457 library outlets. From these totals, the researchers used SPSS Complex Samples software to draw the sample for the study. The sample had to provide the study team with the ability to analyze survey data at the state and national levels along the poverty and metropolitan status strata listed above. The study team drew a sample with replacement of 6,979 outlets. Finally, the sample drawn used a 95% confidence interval for purposes of data analysis.

The study team developed the questions on the survey through an iterative and collaborative effort involving the researchers, representatives of the funding agencies, and members of the Study Advisory Committee. The study team pre-tested the initial surveys with the project's advisory committee, public librarians, and the state data coordinators of the state library agencies and revised the survey on the basis of their comments and suggestions. The survey asked respondents to answer questions about specific library branches and about the library system to which each respondent branch belonged. Respondents answered the survey between November 2006 and February 2007. After several follow-up reminders and other strategies, the survey received a total of 4,027 responses, for a response rate of 57.7%.

There were numerous goals for the data collected. As a result, the findings from the study have wide implications for public libraries, funding agencies, policymakers, and library patrons. At the most general level, these types of findings can provide a picture of the state of technology in the field (Bertot, McClure, and Jaeger 2005). These findings also raise many significant public policy issues related to information and communication technologies in public libraries (Jaeger et al. 2006). As this book details, the findings from the study also reveal a great deal about the social roles of public libraries in terms of the provision of Internet access and related technologies.

The findings of this research are not the only element of the study relevant to this discussion. The importance of this research in terms of public libraries has grown along with the increases in Internet connectivity. Understanding the social roles of public libraries now hinges on understanding the role of Internet access within the library, the degree to which Internet access does or does not support traditional public library social roles, and the growing impacts of Internet-enabled social roles. The level of connectivity and other issues related to Internet access within the library have become the best measure of many aspects of public libraries, including the social roles they are attempting to fulfill.

Some questions from the 2004–2007 studies have explored the ways public libraries are positioning themselves to play certain roles within the information society by prioritizing Internet access. These questions were designed to provide insight into the ways the provision of Internet access and services is having an impact on the established social roles of public libraries. Unless otherwise noted, the data in this chapter—as well as in chapters 4 and 5—come from the 2004–2007 studies (Bertot, McClure, and Jaeger 2005; Bertot, McClure, et al. 2006; Bertot et al. 2007).

Although the social roles of the public library in the networked society are clearly still rapidly evolving, there are identifiable trends in library activities and policies that show them claiming certain social roles in terms of the Internet and avoiding others. In many cases, these social roles are manifested in the ways libraries are

- providing and prioritizing Internet access
- providing Internet training for patrons
- training librarians to use the Internet
- ensuring access to e-government information and services
- providing community support in emergencies
- limiting access to the Internet

Many strands are woven together within these manifestations, including public policy; target audiences for libraries; the search for high-quality access; federal, state, and local government limitations placed on libraries; the use of space within libraries; political pressures on information access; and economic pressures on technology and training. Many of the uses and activities related to the Internet, however, do not seem to be sufficiently linked to using the new social role of Internet access provider as a support mechanism for the established social roles.

In general, the data from recent studies show that libraries have made the provision of Internet access to their communities a top priority, if not the top priority (Bertot, McClure, and Jaeger 2008). Many different groups now rely on the public library to ensure Internet access. In everyday contexts, public libraries guarantee access to and assistance in using the Internet for individuals with no other means of access to computing technology as well as individuals with other access to computing technology and the Internet who nevertheless rely on the public library as a preferred place of access because of its capacity and support (Bertot, Jaeger, et al. 2006a, 2006b).

Many public libraries are maintaining or increasing their technology budgets, their Internet connectivity speeds, and the number of hours library Internet access is available to the public. These efforts demonstrate that public libraries are committed to the provision of Internet access and are making such access a primary part of their services to patrons and local communities.

In many communities, public libraries have no choice but to make public access to the Internet a key social role. A particularly significant finding from the 2007 study was that 73.1% of libraries are the only provider of free Internet access in their communities, as can be seen in table 2. In short, this means that public libraries truly are the guarantors of public access to the Internet in the United States. A mere 17.4% of communities have another public-access point to rely on beyond the library. In three-quarters of the communities in the country, residents have only the public library to ensure public access, meaning that any diminution in the quality or capacity of Internet access in any of these public libraries would negatively affect the access of the entire community (Bertot, McClure, and Jaeger 2008).

At this time, virtually every public library in the United States is connected to the Internet and provides free public access. In 1994 only 20.9% of libraries were connected to the Internet; in 2007, 99.7% were connected. The connectivity rate over the past several years has increased from 98.7% in 2002 to 99.6% in 2004 to 98.9% in 2006 (Bertot, McClure, and Jaeger 2005; Jaeger, Bertot, and McClure 2007). This dramatic increase over a period of a little more than ten years from little over a fifth to virtually all libraries being connected to the Internet demonstrates the prioritization that has been given to the Internet by libraries. As table 3 demonstrates, the connectivity rate of public libraries over the past several years has effectively reached its saturation point, with only a small percentage of libraries remaining unconnected.

Almost every library with an Internet connection offers free public access. As table 4 shows, 99.1% of libraries now offer public access to the Internet. Thus, public libraries seem universally to perceive that providing Internet access is now an essential aspect of their social roles. Further, in 2007, 54.2% of public library branches offered wireless Internet access, a dramatic increase from 36.7% in 2006.

Guaranteeing this access is becoming increasingly difficult for public libraries, however; they seem to be reaching a plateau in the amount of computers and access they can provide given financial, staffing, physical, and other constraints (McClure, Jaeger, and Bertot 2007). The answers to several questions over the past few years

Table 2 Public Libraries as the Only Provider of Free Public Internet Access (2007)

Free Public Access	%
Yes	73.1
No	17.4
Do not know	5.3
Other	2.8

Source: Bertot et al. (2007).

Table 3   Public Libraries Connected to the Internet by Metropolitan Status and Poverty (2007)

	Poverty Level			
Metropolitan Status	Low (%)	Medium (%)	High (%)	Overall (%)
Urban	100.0	100.0	100.0	100.0
Suburban	99.8	100.0	100.0	99.8
Rural	99.7	98.2	85.7	99.5
Overall	99.8	99.3	97.6	99.7

Source: Bertot et al. (2007).

Table 4   Connected Public Libraries Providing Public Access to the Internet by Metropolitan Status and Poverty

	Poverty Level			
Metropolitan Status	Low (%)	Medium (%)	High (%)	Overall (%)
Urban	99.6	99.4	97.1	99.4
Suburban	99.3	100.0	100.0	99.3
Rural	99.1	98.2	85.7	98.9
Overall	99.2	99.0	95.3	99.1

Source: Bertot et al. (2007).

indicate that public libraries may have reached a plateau along key infrastructure measures of Internet workstations and bandwidth. In contrast to the long-term trend of increases, several important data points have held steady or decreased:

- In 2007, 32.9% of connected public library branches had connection speeds of 769 kbps–1.5 Mbps, down slightly from 34.4% in 2006.
- In 2007, 29.2% had connection speeds of greater than 1.5 Mbps, compared to 28.9% in 2006.
- Bandwidth speed has decreased slightly, with 62.1% of public library branches having connection speeds of greater than 769 kbps in 2007 compared to 63.3% in 2006.
- The average number of public-access Internet workstations in 2007 was 10.7, a number that has not changed significantly since 2002 (2002: 10.8; 2004: 10.4; 2006: 10.7).

Table 5   Sufficiency of Public-Access Internet Workstations (2007)

Sufficiency of Public-Access Workstations	%
There are consistently fewer public Internet workstations than patrons who wish to use them throughout a typical day.	18.7
There are fewer public Internet workstations than patrons who wish to use them at different times throughout a typical day.	58.8
There are always sufficient public Internet workstations available for patrons who wish to use them during a typical day.	21.9

Source: Bertot et al. (2007).

Table 6   Public Library Outlet Public-Access Internet Connection
Adequacy (2007)

Adequacy of Public-Access Internet Connection	%
The connection speed is insufficient to meet patron needs.	15.9
The connection speed is sufficient to meet patron needs at some times.	36.4
The connection speed is sufficient to meet patron needs at all times.	43.6
Don't know	1.1

Source: Bertot et al. (2007).

The fact that the average number of workstations has remained steady from 2002 to 2007 raises questions about the ability of public libraries to meet patron needs for Internet access. If considerations of space, cost, staff, and telecommunications availability are creating a level of access beyond which libraries cannot collectively reach, then it appears that libraries may have reached an infrastructure plateau.

This plateau means that providing adequate service is getting harder as more patrons expect to use computers in libraries and the services they want to use grow more complicated and require greater bandwidth. As shown in table 5, only 21.9% of libraries can always meet demand for public Internet access. The vast majority of libraries have insufficient workstations to meet patron demand part (58.8%) or all of the day (18.7%).

Given the limited sufficiency of public workstations in many libraries, it is not surprising that fewer than half (43.6%) of libraries think their connection speed is sufficient to meet patron needs at all times, as is shown in table 6. As the content and services on the Internet, particularly social networking and other Web 2.0 technologies as well as digital media content, become more complicated and require greater bandwidth, the connection speeds patrons require from public library Internet access will continue to increase. If libraries do not begin to increase connection speeds and add, replace, or upgrade workstations, the number of libraries able to say that their "connection speed is sufficient to

Table 7   Factors Influencing Replacement of Public-Access Internet Workstations (2007)

Factors Influencing Workstation Replacement Decision	%
Cost factors	84.1
Maintenance, upgrade, and general upkeep	37.8
Availability of staff	28.1
Other	13.2

Source: Bertot et al. (2007).

Note: Does not total to 100% because respondents could select more than one option.

Table 8   Factors Influencing Addition of Public-Access Internet Workstations in 2006 and 2007

Factors Influencing Workstation Addition Decisions	2006 (%)	2007 (%)
Space limitations	79.9	76.1
Cost factors	72.6	72.6
Maintenance, upgrade, and general upkeep	38.8	26.3
Staff time	19.5	16.1
Inadequate bandwidth to support additional workstations	8.8	13.0
Availability of electrical outlets, cabling, or other infrastructure	—*	31.2
Current number of workstations meets patron needs	20.7	13.9
Other	4.5	2.6

Source: Bertot, McClure et al. (2006); Bertot et al. (2007).

Note: Does not total to 100% because respondents could select more than one option.

*Not asked on the 2006 survey.

meet patron needs at all times" or that "there are always sufficient public Internet workstations available for patrons who wish to use them during a typical day" will likely decline in the near future.

The factors driving this infrastructure plateau can also be seen in the reasons libraries opt not to replace or upgrade workstations in the library. Table 7 indicates that the overwhelming reason for decisions not to replace workstations is cost (84.1%) followed by maintenance, upgrade, and general upkeep (37.8%), availability of staff (28.1%), and other (13.2%).

Table 8 offers greater insight into the potential reasons for the infrastructure plateau. Between 2006 and 2007, space limitations and cost factors held

Table 9   Factors Affecting Public Library Outlet's Ability to Provide Public-Access Internet Connection (2007)

Factors Affecting Connection	%
There is no space for workstations and/or necessary equipment.	48.2
The library does not have access to adequate telecommunications services.	27.1
The library cannot afford the necessary equipment.	24.7
The library does not have the staff necessary to install, maintain, and/or upgrade the necessary technology.	18.7
The library cannot afford the recurring telecommunications costs.	14.3
The library does not control its access to Internet services.	11.3
The library building cannot support the necessary infrastructure (power, cabling, other).	10.9
There is no interest within the local community in connecting the library to the Internet.	3.2
There is no interest among library staff or management in connecting the library to the Internet.	—
Other	29.3

Source: Bertot et al. (2007).

Note: Does not total to 100% because respondents could select more than one option.

steady as the predominant reasons preventing libraries from adding workstation capacity. Technical and telecommunications infrastructure problems were significant as well. Also telling is the fact that the number of libraries responding that "the current number of workstations meets the needs of our patrons" dropped from 20.7% in 2006 to 13.9% in 2007, yet few libraries were adding or replacing workstations to meet patron needs in 2007.

Table 9 focuses on the small number of libraries that still do not provide free public library Internet access. Almost half of them (48.2%) cited a lack of space for workstations and other necessary equipment as the primary factor affecting their ability to provide access, while another 10.9% reported that the building could not support the necessary infrastructure. Lack of access to telecommunications services (27.1%) was the second most frequently cited reason. Lack of funding for telecommunications costs (14.3%) or for staffing (18.7%) were also problems for some libraries. The reasons cited by the small number of libraries that do not provide access echo the barriers many of the libraries that do provide access face in trying to increase the services they provide—cost, telecommunications infrastructure, staffing, and physical space. The roots of the infrastructure plateau may be reflected in the barriers to access still encountered by libraries that have yet to make the Internet available.

Despite the level of priority accorded to the Internet in most libraries, many public libraries clearly must deal with sizable economic, staffing, physical, and other constraints in the provision of Internet access and related technologies. Even within these economic constraints, however, the technology upgrade schedules maintained by public libraries are worthy of discussion. In 2004, nearly 70% of libraries had no set upgrade schedule for hardware, 77.4% had no set upgrade schedule for software, and 96.4% had no set upgrade schedule for connection speed. Only approximately 50% of libraries had a public-access workstation replacement schedule, and only 39% of libraries with such a schedule were able to maintain it. This lack of upgrade schedules may be heavily shaped by economic realities, but it also demonstrates that public libraries have not fully assimilated the significance of providing Internet access to their established social roles. The predominant lack of upgrade schedules signifies an insufficient embrace of the social responsibilities and opportunities that accompany the provision of Internet access.

Paying limited attention to the technological necessities that accompany providing Internet access, such as upgrading technologies, may have significant implications for how society perceives the Internet access provided by public libraries. If public libraries generally have outdated hardware, software, and connection speeds and lack a sensible pattern for upgrading their technology, patrons may come to view the public library as an unreliable or outdated provider of Internet access. Clearly, libraries cannot upgrade their Internet-related technologies every year. Not keeping technologies current at least every few years, however, may lead to a perception that the Internet access in libraries is inadequate. This situation may lead patrons to seek other avenues for Internet access, costing libraries in terms of library usage and perceived social roles and value.

4

Internet Services and Training in Social Roles of Public Libraries

Training activities have long been an important part of the ways public libraries have served their patrons and their communities. Over the years, such activities have ranged from training for job-seeking skills to training to help new immigrants learn life skills they would need in the United States. As computers became more commonplace, training patrons in the use of computers became a common function of libraries. A natural outgrowth of that has been the important role libraries now play in providing Internet-enabled technology training to patrons and library professionals.

INTERNET TRAINING FOR THE COMMUNITY

A key social role of public libraries and a primary expectation from patrons related to the Internet is the provision of technology services and training, including free training on how to use the Internet and a range of services—subscription and staff developed—for patrons to access. As table 10 indicates, the types of public-access Internet services public libraries most frequently offer are licensed databases (85.6%), homework resources (68.1%), digital reference or virtual reference services (57.7%), e-books (38.3%), and audio content such as podcasts and audio books (38%). Beyond the options listed in this question on the survey, libraries mentioned many other types of services, including community information, interlibrary loans, genealogy databases, and obituary indexes.

Libraries were also asked to indicate the Internet services they provided to their communities in terms of content. Table 11 reveals that many librar-

Table 10   Types of Public-Access Internet Services in Public Libraries (2007)

Internet Services	%
Licensed databases	85.6
Homework resources	68.1
Digital reference/virtual reference	57.7
E-books	38.3
Audio content (podcasts, audio books, other)	38.0
Online instructional courses/tutorials	34.4
Digitized special collections (letters, postcards, documents, other)	21.1
Video content	16.6
Video conferencing	4.3
Other	3.8

Source: Bertot et al. (2007).

Note: Does not total to 100% because respondents could select more than one option.

ies are working to use the Internet to provide educational resources. The top answer and three of the next five answers involved educational impacts—education resources and databases for K–12 students (67.7%), adult/continuing education (27.5%), higher education (21.4%), and home schooling (14.5%). The second and third most common answers related to providing services for job seekers (44%) and providing computer and Internet skills training (29.8%).

Table 12 identifies the major impacts of information technology training provided to patrons by public libraries. Providing information literacy skills was the most commonly reported impact of the technology training (45.7%); providing technology skills training were the second (39.4%) and third (37.6%) most frequent. Helping students with school and homework assignments was reported by 35.2% of libraries, but, curiously, facilitating local economic development (2.3%) and helping local business owners (1.7%) were rarely cited as impacts despite the importance of local tax revenue to funding the public library. Another point of interest is that 23.8% of libraries offer no training at all.

The target audiences of the information technology training services being offered to patrons reveal much about the social roles public libraries are trying to fulfill in relation to the Internet. Among the wide variety of potential audiences, the most common groups being trained to use the Internet and related technologies were seniors (57.3%), people without home access (52.6%), and adults seeking continuing education (51.2%). The groups that are being emphasized in targeted Internet training are all populations for which such training seems valuable. Compelling cases could, however, be made for targeting other groups.

Table 11   Content of Public-Access Internet Services Critical to the Role of the Public Library (2007)

Public Internet Services	%
Provide education resources and databases for K–12 students	67.7
Provide services for job seekers	44.0
Provide computer and Internet skills training	29.8
Provide education resources and databases for adult/continuing education students	27.5
Provide education resources and databases for students in higher education	21.4
Provide education resources and databases for homeschooling	14.5
Provide information about the library's community	14.1
Provide services to new citizens and residents	12.7
Provide access to federal government documents	8.3
Provide access to local public and local government documents	6.9
Provide information for college applicants	5.4
Provide information for local economic development	3.9
Provide information or databases regarding investments	3.2
Provide information about state and local business opportunities	2.9
Provide information for local business marketing	1.0
Other	12.4

Source: Bertot et al. (2007).

Note: Does not total to 100% because respondents could select more than one option.

People without Internet access at work, for example, make sense as an audience for the same reasons that people without home access do. A person who lacks access at work may or may not have other opportunities to learn about and use Internet technologies at home or in an educational setting. Underrepresented or socially marginalized populations, including immigrants and resident aliens, non-English-speaking populations, and persons with disabilities, would benefit greatly from focused training offered in public libraries, particularly in terms of accessing government information and services (Jaeger and Thompson 2003, 2004). Also, the limited levels of training that target students at certain levels of education may be missing important groups that could benefit from training in the public library and become lifelong users of the public library.

Table 12   Impacts of Public Library Information Technology Training for
Patrons (2007)

Impacts of Training	%
Provides information literacy skills	45.7
Offers technology training to those who would otherwise not have any	39.4
Provides general technology skills	37.6
Helps students with their school assignments and schoolwork	35.2
No training offered	23.8
Helps patrons complete job applications	21.5
Helps users access and use electronic government services and resources	19.9
Facilitates local economic development	2.3
Helps business owners understand and use technology and/or information resources	1.7
Other	2.8

Source: Bertot et al. (2007).

Note: Does not total to 100% because respondents could select more than one option.

Providing Internet training targeted toward groups that are typically marginalized within society would simultaneously better integrate these persons into society and create new patrons for libraries. Many people who rely on educational settings for Internet access will not have it when they are finished with school, either at home or at work, making the library a likely provider of Internet service, particularly if they already think of the library as a source of Internet resources.

Training targeted at such groups would help increase the number and diversity of patrons of public libraries, but offering training targeted to other specific groups—such as local businesses, local government, and local service organizations—might actually help increase the position of libraries within communities. Offering training that targets local businesses, local government, and local service organizations could help members of those groups introduce, increase, or improve the use of the Internet in these professional and government contexts. Given the growing importance of the Internet in government and professional contexts, many people in these groups may be searching for reliable outlets from which to receive training. These types of connections could increase the importance of the library to these local organizations as a source of information and technology access. These connections could also be a great benefit to the library itself, since more community leaders in government and business would have an improved understanding of the importance of the public library and what it provides to the community. At a time when many libraries are pressed for funding, finding ways that the Internet can serve as a connection to other community organizations could be very significant for libraries when local funds are allocated by governments and when local businesses consider making charitable donations to the library.

Internet Training for Library Staff

Most public libraries provide Internet training to members of the library staff, with such training coming from libraries, consortia, state libraries, vendors, volunteers, and other sources. The vast majority of public libraries—86.4%—provide Internet training to the staff. The topics most frequently covered in these training sessions include using online databases (59.9%), general computer software use (54.5%), online searching (51.3%), general Internet use (51.2%), and helping the public use the Internet (49.5%). These areas of focus are all obviously of value to librarians and the patrons they serve. The fact that fewer than half of libraries instruct librarians in helping the public use the Internet does seem curious, though, since nearly all libraries offer public Internet access. Further, in several areas important to the social roles of the public library as a marketplace of ideas, training for staff is limited.

The provision of online government information and services to patrons is a useful example. The federal government is increasingly relying on the public library as an access point by which all citizens can reach e-government websites (Bertot, Jaeger, et al. 2006a, 2006b; Jaeger and Fleischmann 2007). This reliance is based on the Telecommunications Act of 1996, the E-government Act of 2002, individual state policy instruments, and other policies that view public libraries as a place where all citizens are able to access e-government if they have no other means of access (Jaeger et al. 2006). Based on the 2007 *Public Libraries and the Internet* data, however, the importance accorded to e-government by libraries does not match the importance of libraries to e-government. Only 27.9% of public libraries train librarians to search for and use federal government information, and 26.3% of public libraries train librarians to search for and use local government information. Though the federal government may be envisioning public libraries as the universal access point in society for e-government, the training of librarians indicates that most libraries are not prepared to serve as society's gateway to e-government. Part of the reason for this situation may be that the responsibilities related to e-government are being given to libraries without sufficient funds to support additional training for staff to assist in these services. Although the E-rate program provides libraries with substantial financial support for several aspects of technology, it does not include funding for related staff training (Jaeger, Bertot, et al. 2007; Jaeger, McClure, and Bertot 2005).

Another important training issue is related to law and policy. Given all the diverse policies and legal issues associated with the Internet, it is surprising that only 15.4% of public libraries provide staff with training related to professional responsibility and the Internet. The Internet is a complex medium when it comes to laws and policies that might affect usage, including thorny issues of copyright, intellectual property, and fair use. Further, public policy, through federal laws such as the Children's Internet Protection Act (CIPA) and the USA PATRIOT Act, is placing librarians in a position where they must be aware of significant issues of law that can govern Internet usage in the library (Jaeger and Burnett 2005; Jaeger, Bertot, and McClure 2003, 2004; Jaeger and McClure 2004; Jaeger et al. 2004, 2005, 2006). Many state and local governments also have laws and policies of which librarians must be aware. Overall, these laws mold a concept of "proper" Internet usage in many contexts within the library. For librarians to lack a full understanding of these laws places the librarians, libraries, and their patrons at legal risk or liability. It also creates a situation in which libraries may not be able to meet the responsibilities given to them under the law.

A third key issue is the lack of focus on technology planning and management (21.7%) in the training of librarians in relation to the Internet. Because providing Internet access is now a major element of the social roles of public libraries, Internet access seems likely to be a long-term part of the services offered. The relative lack of training for librarians in terms of technology planning and management indicates that public libraries have not fully accepted how important the provision of Internet access is to their social roles and that it will likely continue to be so. Given the number of factors that can affect the provision of Internet access in libraries, the importance of technology planning and management is considerable, whether it be fiscal and budgeting matters, quality of access, types of services being developed and offered, or determinations of how to address policy issues such as legislatively mandated filtering.

5

Policy and the Internet in
Social Roles of Public Libraries

Public libraries are affected by a wide range of policy instruments from local, state, and federal governments, including an array of legislation, executive orders, judicial rulings, guidelines and regulations, rulemaking, agency memos, signing statements, agency circulars, and other types of official statements (McClure and Jaeger, forthcoming). Public policy can have far-ranging impacts on what libraries must do and what they can do, but three areas of library services heavily shaped by public policy are possible only as a result of the Internet access and training libraries are expected to provide: emergency community support, access to e-government, and Internet filtering.

Community Support in Emergencies

In recent years, through a confluence of policies and events, public libraries and the Internet access they provide have taken on increasing importance as community support structures during emergencies (Bertot, Jaeger, et al. 2006a, 2006b; Jaeger, Langa, et al. 2006). In the aftermath of the hurricanes that struck during the devastating 2004 and 2005 seasons, public libraries and the Internet access they provided were relied on by communities for many vital information roles (Bertot, Jaeger, et al. 2006a, 2006b):

- Finding and communicating with dispersed and displaced family members and friends
- Completing FEMA forms, which are online only, and insurance claims

- Searching for news about conditions in the area from which they had evacuated
- Obtaining information about the condition of their homes or places of work, including checking news sites and satellite maps
- Helping emergency service providers find information and connect to the Internet

The level of assistance was significant—one Mississippi library completed more than 45,000 FEMA applications for patrons in the first month after Katrina struck—despite the fact that the libraries were not specifically prepared to offer such a service and few library systems had planned for this type of situation (Bertot, Jaeger, et al. 2006a). And public libraries played many more roles than providing access to and assistance in finding information, including these (Jaeger, Langa, et al. 2006):

- Helping communities prepare by creating and distributing emergency preparedness guides, both printed and web-based; conducting disaster information workshops; and running volunteer coordination programs.
- Providing emergency information by staffing emergency operations centers and local government offices; answering phone calls; answering e-mail questions; conducting interactive chat services; handling communications in and out of the city; creating community contact centers for community members to reestablish contact; and addressing inquiries from other parts of the country and from around the world about the conditions in the area or about particular residents.
- Giving shelter by managing and staffing shelters for evacuees in both library buildings and other buildings; providing city employees and relief workers with places to sleep; and housing city command centers for disasters (e.g., police, fire, public works).
- Providing physical aid by cooking and distributing meals; distributing water, ice, meals ready to eat, tarps, and bug spray; registering people with the "blue roof program;" providing hookups to recharge electronics and communication devices; filling water bottles; letting people use library refrigerators for food and medication; and unloading truckloads of relief supplies.
- Caring for community members in need by assisting with the completion of FEMA forms, insurance documents, and other paperwork; caring for special-needs and elderly evacuees; working as translators for evacuees; running day camps for children when schools were closed and for children of city employees who had to work unusual hours; holding programs in shelters; providing library materials to evacuees in shelters; establishing temporary libraries in shelters; and sending bookmobiles to devastated areas.
- Working with relief organizations by assisting FEMA, Red Cross, and Army Corps of Engineers personnel in their duties, including providing their personnel with a place to meet with residents; providing meeting

spaces for relief and rescue personnel; providing relief personnel a place to use the Internet, e-mail, and telephones; giving temporary library cards to relief workers; and helping FEMA personnel identify local areas that suffered major damage.

- Cleaning up the damage after the storms by securing city buildings before storms; checking structures for damage; cleaning up debris; and restoring damaged government structures.

Given these diverse and enormously important social roles and the technology provided in emergencies, it is clearly necessary for libraries to have well-developed emergency plans. Further, the performance of public libraries during the aftermath of major hurricanes such as Katrina, Ivan, Rita, and Wilma cemented the public perception that they will be ready to aid their communities during emergencies (Jaeger and Fleischmann 2007; Jaeger, Langa, et al. 2006).

Table 13 shows the roles public libraries expect to play in the event of disaster or emergency situations. Nearly one-third (31.9%) noted that their computing and Internet services would be used by the public to access relief services and benefits. Based on the experiences of the 2004 and 2005 hurricane seasons, it is likely that many public libraries in communities that have not recently experienced a major emergency would find their computers used for access to relief services and benefits, even if they did not expect this. Similarly, many more libraries than the 18.5% that indicated they planned to serve as an emergency shelter might be forced into that role, depending on the circumstances of an emergency. The other emergency roles reported by libraries include serving as command and control centers, temporary setups for local businesses, classrooms in the case of public school damage, and evacuation sites for local schools. Unfortunately, many of the libraries that marked "other" also indicated having no disaster plan.

Table 14 shows the degree to which public library systems have established emergency or disaster plans. The highest number of libraries (28.8%) reported that they do not currently have any sort of plan in place and that they are not

Table 13 Disaster/Emergency Roles and Services of the Public Library (2007)

Disaster/Emergency Roles and Services	%
The library's public computing and Internet access services are used by the public to access emergency relief services and benefits.	31.9
The library building serves as an emergency shelter.	18.5
The library staff provide emergency responder services.	7.5
The library's equipment is used by first responders.	6.0
Other	7.8

Source: Bertot et al. (2007).

Note: Does not total to 100% because respondents could select more than one option.

Table 14   Public Library Disaster/Emergency Plans (2007)

Disaster/Emergency Plan	%
There is no current written plan, and one is not in the process of being developed.	28.2
There is no current written plan, but one is in the process of being developed.	21.9
There is a current written plan, but it is more than one year old.	21.9
There is a current written plan.	15.6
The library is involved in disaster and emergency planning activities at the local level (e.g., town, city, county).	15.3
The library's existing plan or plan under development was developed in conjunction with local or other emergency service organizations (e.g., fire, police, disaster relief).	7.3
Do not know	3.2
Other	2.7

Source: Bertot et al. (2007).

Note: Does not total to 100% because respondents could select more than one option.

developing one. Only 15.6% of libraries have a current, up-to-date written plan in place. On a more positive note, 15.3% of libraries are in the process of developing an emergency preparedness plan, and another 21.9% are updating existing plans that are more than a year old. The experiences of public libraries after the hurricanes of 2004 and 2005 should serve as impetus for libraries that still need to develop or update emergency plans. Whether they are prepared or not, public libraries and their Internet access clearly are expected by patrons, communities, and governments to fulfill emergency response, support, and recovery roles.

E-GOVERNMENT ACCESS AND TRAINING

E-government is the provision of government information and services through the online environment, including everything from applying for Medicare prescription drug plans to paying taxes to e-mailing a public official. A new but extremely important social role for public libraries is ensuring that all citizens have access to and assistance using e-government information and services. A significant proportion of the U.S. population—including people who have no other means of access, people who need help using technology, and people who have lower-quality access—rely on the access and trust the assistance available in public libraries to use e-government websites (Jaeger and Fleischmann 2007).

Many federal, state, and local government agencies now direct citizens to the nearest public library for access and help in filing taxes, welfare requests, immigration documents, and numerous other essential government forms

Table 15   E-government Roles and Services of the Public Library (2007)

E-government Roles and Services	%
Staff provide as-needed assistance to patrons for understanding how to access and use government websites, programs, and services.	78.5
Staff provide assistance to patrons applying for or accessing e-government services.	55.0
The library is partnering with government agencies, nonprofit organizations, and others to provide e-government services.	12.8
The library offers training classes regarding the use of government websites, programs, and electronic forms.	8.4
Other	2.1

Source: Bertot et al. (2007).

Note: Does not total to 100% because respondents could select more than one option.

(Bertot, Jaeger, et al. 2006a, 2006b). The vital roles public libraries played in the aftermath of the major hurricanes of 2004 and 2005 by providing access to FEMA forms and other e-government materials essential for emergency response and recovery may have permanently cemented the public and government perception of public libraries as hubs for e-government access (Jaeger, Langa, et al. 2006).

As noted earlier, nearly 75% of the public libraries reported that in their communities the public library is the only source of free public access to the Internet (McClure, Jaeger, and Bertot 2007). This means that public libraries truly are the guarantors of public access to e-government in the United States. In three-quarters of the communities in the country, the residents have only the public library to ensure access to federal, state, and local e-government information and services.

As table 15 indicates, the vast majority of public libraries (78.5%) provide access to and assistance with government websites, programs, and services. Additionally, over half of public library systems (55%) provide assistance to patrons applying for or accessing e-government services, such as taxes or Medicare applications. More advanced forms of e-government assistance, like partnering with government agencies (12.8%) and providing e-government training courses (8.4%), have not yet been as widely embraced by public libraries.

Support of e-government is a social role that will continue to grow in importance for public libraries as more and more government information and services go exclusively online. The public library "is a trusted community-based entity to which individuals turn for help in their online activities—even if they have computers and Internet access at home or elsewhere" (Bertot, Jaeger, et al. 2006a). Citizens seek access to e-government at the public library not only because access is available but also because they know they can get help and trust the help they receive there (Jaeger and Fleischmann 2007). Many individuals who are otherwise confident Internet users seek help at the public library when doing their taxes online or applying for Medicare, among many other daily citizen interactions with e-government. "When people struggle with, become frustrated by, or reject e-government services, they turn to public libraries" (Jaeger and Fleischmann 2007, 42).

Public libraries now must be able to provide patrons with help using a wide range of e-government information and services. At just the level of local government, the most common e-government activities in public libraries include finding court proceedings, submitting local zoning board information, requesting planning permits, searching property and assessor databases, registering students in school, taking driver's education programs, applying for permits, scheduling appointments with government officials, paying fees and taxes, and completing numerous other local government functions online (Jaeger, forthcoming). As with emergency roles, e-government access and assistance are highly significant social roles that patrons, communities, and governments all rely on public libraries to fulfill.

Filtering Internet Access

The filtering of Internet access is one controversial social role that more libraries are assuming, as the federal government, many state and local governments, and many communities look to the library to provide Internet access and prevent minors from reaching certain online content simultaneously. Although a majority of libraries (58.2%) do not use filters on computers, the number using them has been increasing. A significant reason for this increase is that the use of filters is now required for the receipt of funds from certain important federal government programs—E-rate and the Library Services and Technology Act (LSTA)—as a result of CIPA. These funds have been extremely important in the growth of Internet access in libraries; the E-rate program provided public libraries with more than $250 million in funds related to Internet access between 2000 and 2003 (Jaeger, McClure, and Bertot 2005). With this mandate of filtering as a prerequisite to receiving funds that are so vital to affording the provision of Internet access, many public libraries have no choice but to adopt filters. Further, some state governments are considering or have passed even broader filtering requirements for public libraries to receive state funds (Jaeger et al. 2005). The CIPA filtering requirements have also shaped how libraries apply for federal funds.

Because libraries clearly need sources of income for providing computers and connections for Internet access, it would be expected that they apply for every source available. But as table 16 demonstrates, only 51.3% of libraries applied for an E-rate discount in 2007, either directly (39.1%) or through some other organization (12.2%). Thus nearly half of libraries did not apply for these funds, which is a large number considering the importance of funds like E-rate.

For those public library systems receiving E-rate discounts, table 17 illustrates which services those funds are being applied to. A strong majority of systems (83.2%) indicated that funds are going toward telecommunications

Table 16   Percentage of Public Libraries That Applied for an E-rate
Discount (2007)

E-rate Applications	%
Applied	39.1
Another organization applied on the library's behalf	12.2
Did not apply	43.8
Do not know	4.0

Source: Bertot et al. (2007).

Table 17   Percentage of Public Libraries Receiving E-rate Discount by
Category (2007)

E-rate Discount Categories	%
Telecommunications services	83.2
Internet connectivity	52.6
Internal connections cost	9.5

Source: Bertot et al. (2007).

Note: Does not total to 100% because respondents could select more than one option.

services. About half (52.6%) stated that E-rate funds went toward Internet connectivity, and only 9.5% reported the funds going toward internal connection costs. E-rate funds can be an important means of financially supporting Internet access to patrons, especially in terms of telecommunications and connectivity costs. And, as tables 6–8 in chapter 3 reveal, cost is a significant barrier to adding new workstations and replacing existing workstations in public libraries, as well as to offering any Internet access to patrons.

Given that E-rate is one of the few programs offering funds to libraries specifically for Internet-related costs, it seems surprising that only about half of libraries apply for the funds. Table 18 shows the reasons that public library systems did not apply for E-rate discounts. The most common reasons included the application process being too complicated (37.8%), the funding amount not being worth the time required to apply (36%), and the filtering requirements of CIPA being considered unacceptable (33.9%). In fact, a substantial increase can be seen over the previous year in the category of libraries not applying because of CIPA filtering requirements; in 2006, 15.3% libraries did not apply for E-rate because of CIPA (Bertot et al. 2007). Ironically, the libraries that are not applying for E-rate funds because of the requirements of CIPA are being forced to turn down the chance for funding to help pay for the Internet access in order to preserve community access to the Internet.

Table 18   Public Library Reasons for Not Applying for E-rate Discounts (2007)

Reasons	%
The E-rate application process is too complicated.	37.8
Our total E-rate discount is fairly low and not worth the time needed to participate in the program.	36.0
The library did not apply because of the need to comply with CIPA's filtering requirements.	33.9
Other	15.8
The library staff did not feel the library would qualify.	9.8
The library has applied for E-rate in the past but no longer finds it necessary.	9.1
The library receives it as part of a consortium so therefore does not apply individually.	8.4
The library was denied funding in the past.	3.0

Source: Bertot et al. (2007).

Note: Does not total to 100% because respondents could select more than one option.

The legal requirement of employing filters is primarily intended to prevent minors from viewing content that is considered inappropriate by lawmakers. Filtering software can, however, be imprecise, and some programs block much more material than they should, particularly materials related to health and to political issues, and can be difficult for library staff to set and disable (Jaeger, Bertot, and McClure 2004; Jaeger and McClure 2004; Jaeger et al. 2005). Because the filtering requirements place the obligation on adult patrons to request unfiltered access to reach materials that are blocked, many patrons may chose to not have access rather than expose themselves to questions from the library staff about why they wish to use the unfiltered Internet (Jaeger et al. 2005, 2006). Within this context, filters clearly do more than prevent minors from seeing certain types of materials on the Internet. Libraries using these filters may actually be altering their social role as marketplace of ideas by limiting what is available to patrons.

Libraries that opt not to apply for E-rate funds run significant risks of falling behind in their ability to provide sufficient Internet access to meet patron demands (Jaeger, Bertot, et al. 2007). Most libraries are having trouble meeting patron needs, but many of those not applying for E-rate are obviously in a worse position than other libraries. The lack of E-rate funding for some libraries is contributing to growing disparities in the amount and quality of Internet access available to library patrons in different regions of the country (Jaeger, Bertot, et al. 2007). For example, the average number of workstations varies significantly across the states and by regions of the country. As figure 4 demonstrates, states in the Southwest, Southeast, parts of the Midwest, and

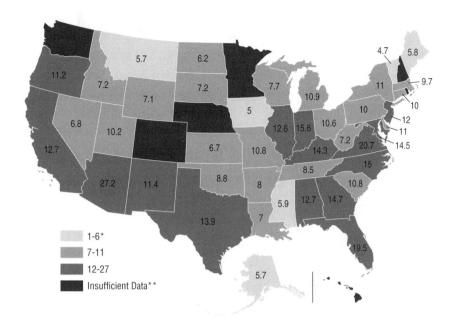

Figure 4   Average number of public library public-access Internet workstations by state, 2007

Source: McClure, Jaeger, and Bertot (2007).

*The value for each state represents the speed chosen by at least 50% of the responses.

**Response rate from this state is too low.

Midatlantic, along with California and Oregon, tend to have the highest average number of public-access workstations available for patron use.

Rather than provide access to all of the content available on the Internet, libraries with filters are providing access to only a certain spectrum of the content, with particular limitations on content related to personal health and political issues. With the limitations created by filters, the perceived social role of a library as provider of Internet access may become modified in the minds of patrons and other members of the community. Even though filtering requirements are being imposed externally on libraries as a government and community expectation, many patrons may see the filters as undermining their expectations of free access to the Internet. The perception may begin to shift toward what the library will not allow patrons to access, whether real or imagined, rather than on content to which the library does provide access. As a result, filters in libraries have great potential to undermine the social role of the library as marketplace of ideas, both in perception and in actuality, while emphasizing a different social role as online monitor and arbiter of community values.

6

Patron, Community, and Government Expectations and Professional Values

A key indicator of the extent to which the provision of Internet access and training by public libraries has altered their social roles is demonstrated in the expectations for such access and training by patrons, communities, and governments. The data detailed in previous chapters show a clear expectation by patrons that libraries will be able to meet their Internet needs; so many people rely on libraries for access and training that libraries are having a difficult time keeping pace. In emergencies, individuals and whole communities count directly on the public library to provide a wide range of assistance. Patrons, communities, and government agencies all rely on the library to ensure access to and assistance with e-government. Many of these expectations are tied not only to libraries having the Internet access but to the trust that has developed in public libraries.

Libraries have come to earn the trust of their communities because of four obligations librarians strive to meet: to provide user-centered service, to help users actively, to connect information seekers to unexplored information sources, and to take the goal of helping users as a professional duty that is controlled first and foremost by the library user (Carr 2003). Simultaneously, because of their traditional defense of commonly accepted and popular values such as free access to and exchange of information, providing a diverse range of materials and perspectives to users from across society, and opposition to government intrusions into personal reading habits, public libraries have come to be seen by members of the populace as a trusted source of information in the community (Jaeger and Burnett 2005).

Former ALA president Michael Gorman has argued for a direct link between the values of libraries and the trust the public has for libraries, stating that one important mission for ensuring the survival of libraries and librarianship is "assuring the bond of trust between the library and the society we serve by demonstrating our stewardship and commitment, thus strengthening the mutuality of the interests of librarians and the broader community" (2000, 66). Further, a 2006 study conducted by Public Agenda found that "public libraries seem almost immune to the distrust that is associated with so many other institutions" (Public Agenda 2006, 11).

In specific terms of the Internet, the public library "is a trusted community-based entity to which individuals turn for help in their online activities—even if they have computers and Internet access at home or elsewhere" (Bertot, Jaeger, et al. 2006a). In the large-scale national Public Agenda survey (2006), 64% of respondents, including both users and nonusers of public libraries, asserted that providing public access to the Internet should be one of the highest priorities for public libraries. Thus, trust in public libraries seems to carry over from other library services to provision of Internet access and training, reinforcing the expectation that access and assistance are always available in libraries. That users who have other access to the Internet still rely on public libraries for access and assistance is indicative of the depth of social expectations of Internet access in public libraries.

In fact, the combination of Internet access, availability of help, trust of the library, and clear successes of libraries in helping communities recover from disasters has resulted in expectations from patrons and communities in which the Internet has a central function, if not the central function, of public libraries. For most patrons, walking into a library and finding no Internet access would be as disconcerting as finding no print materials (Jaeger and Burnett 2005). This attitude has also carried over to federal, state, and local government agencies that now count on public libraries to ensure computer, Internet, and e-government access for citizens. For example, government agencies are quick to recommend to their clients that they use the public library resources to engage in e-government services (McClure, Jaeger, and Bertot 2007):

- *Recovery Times,* a FEMA publication, suggests residents who need to get help from FEMA "visit a public library to use a computer free of charge" (www.fema.gov/pdf/rt/rt_1609_120605.pdf).
- The Federal Code of Regulation from the Department of Labor (Title 20, Vol. 3, Part 655, Subpart H, Sec. 655.720) states that the filing and processing of labor condition applications must be done online, unless documentation can be provided that Internet access is not available through the employer and "there is no publicly available Internet access, at public libraries or elsewhere, within a reasonable distance of the employer" (http://a257.g.akamaitech.net/7/257/2422/10apr20061500/edocket.access.gpo.gov/cfr_2006/aprqtr/pdf/20cfr655.720.pdf).
- The first step in the *10 Steps to Help You Fill Your Grocery Bag through the Food Stamp Program* is the use of the Internet Tool. Stated under the

Internet Tool is "your local library usually has computers you can use" (www.fns.usda.gov/fsp/applicant_recipients/10steps.pdf).

- The Florida Department of Environmental Protection released a memo involving the use of the People First System for the posting of job vacancies, which states, "Since this system is Internet based, employees can apply for vacancies from any computer, such as a home computer, public library computer, or computers at the Agency for Workforce's Workforce Centers" (www.dep.state.fl.us/admin/forms/Personnel_Forms/DEP_54-804.doc)

There are other examples, and all clearly demonstrate the expectation among federal, state, and local government agencies that public libraries will meet the nation's needs for the provision of, access to, and assistance with e-government services. Ultimately, public libraries have been so successful in providing Internet access and assistance that the social expectation of these services now extends from individual patrons to entire communities to government agencies.

Several studies validate the findings from the 2007 *Public Libraries and the Internet* study summarized above. Focus groups conducted by the ALA in 2006–7 identify a range of public expectations for Internet-enabled library services (American Library Association and Information Institute, 2007), including

- e-mail
- job applications and professional resources
- homework and education-related services
- e-commerce—being able to conduct personal business electronically
- social networking applications such as MySpace, YouTube, and Flickr
- e-government
- downloading software, media, and other applications/programs
- accessing complex databases or other electronic resources

These do not include a range of specific examples of expectations such as solving personal medical issues with current online information, using an Ask-a-Librarian online service, or youth uses of gaming software. Of interest is the finding that users of the public library now expect to find these and other Internet-related services and applications in the library, to not have to wait to access these services, to have adequate time to use the workstation and not be "timed out," to have services of adequate bandwidth, and to have available trained and knowledgeable staff to assist them—both on-site and remotely.

Another interesting user expectation documented in various studies is the growing expectation for free public wireless connectivity (Weingarten et al. 2007). As data presented earlier show, the extent of wireless connections being provided by public libraries has increased considerably. Indeed, data clearly show that community members often expect wireless connections from the public library as they sit in a nearby parking area—so they do not actually have to come into the library. Thus, the expectation now is that the public library can provide free public access as some commercial coffee shops and other organizations do. More important, perhaps, is the expectation that the public library will provide current, easy to use, and accessible information technology, making some public librarians Internet/technology managers—with skills and knowledge not needed in 1987.

The current values of libraries and of the profession of librarianship have also clearly been shaped by the increasing importance of the Internet in library services. Gorman (1997, 2000, 2005) has written extensively about what he sees as the library values that demonstrate the core and enduring values of the profession. According to Gorman, values should provide a foundation for inter-action and mutual understanding among members of a profession. But he also believes that values should not be viewed as immutable. Instead, they should act as flexible ideals that evolve in line with the changing times. Gorman sees eight central values of librarianship as particularly salient at present: steward-ship, service, intellectual freedom, rationalism, literacy and learning, equity of access to recorded knowledge and information, privacy, and democracy. Many of these values are tied closely to the Internet.

Frances Groen (2007) has echoed Gorman's sentiments, arguing that one of the major limitations of LIS programs is their lack of attention to values. She argues that LIS programs place the vast majority of their educational emphasis on what librarians do and how they do it, virtually ignoring the reasons why they do what they do and why such activities are important to individuals, com-munities, and society in general. Groen identifies three fundamental library values—access to information, universal literacy, and preservation of cultural heritage—all of which, she argues, are also characteristics of liberal democratic societies. This argument parallels the observation that increases in information access within a society are essential to increasing the inclusiveness of the dem-ocratic process in that society (Smith 1995). All of these values are enhanced by the Internet-enabled library.

Library historian Toni Samek (2001) has focused on another aspect of library values that is no longer as strongly emphasized—attempts to achieve "neutrality" in libraries. Neutrality was often advocated as a cherished value, in the sense of providing equal access to all information and sources. Libraries were, however, more likely to emphasize mainstream information sources and thus privilege them over alternative sources. Not only has the value of neutral-ity been problematic in terms of how it has been implemented and mobilized in public libraries in the 1960s and 1970s, but also it is indeed perhaps impos-sible to ever achieve in reality (Scott, Richards, and Martin 1990). The fact that neither Gorman nor Groen includes neutrality in their listings of fundamen-tal library values demonstrates how library values have continued to evolve as public libraries have developed as social institutions.

As library values have developed, they have also affected the service roles of and expectations for public libraries in their communities. The values of librari-anship have been encoded in the ALA's Library Bill of Rights, which strongly asserts the values of equal access and service for all patrons, nondiscrimina-tion, diversity of viewpoint, and resistance to censorship and other abridgments of freedom of expression. The study of the role of values in libraries is essential, especially given the increasing role of technology in public libraries (Fleischmann 2007). Current library values are another aspect that must be considered in understanding the current social roles of and expectations for public libraries. The rise of the importance of the Internet in library roles and expectations helps shape library values, while, in turn, libraries' values help establish what roles libraries attempt to employ the Internet for.

The data and ideas presented in this chapter suggest that the expectations for library services from community members, library users, remote users, and federal, state, and local governments have changed significantly since the 1987 publication of eight social roles for public libraries. Simultaneously, the values of librarianship have evolved to keep pace with the changes in expectations and in technology. The extent to which the Internet and the range of digital services and resources made available through the public library have evolved since 1987 is truly expansive. Yet the social roles and the service responses articulated by the PLA have changed little.

7

Implications of Internet-Enabled Roles

The sizable importance of the Internet in libraries has significant implications for the roles of libraries. The Internet access, services, and training are leading to new Internet-enabled roles for libraries. These same changes are also leading to changes to the established roles of libraries. Further, libraries face new challenges in reconciling the new Internet-enabled roles with the traditional roles that have served to define the public library.

THE NEW ROLES

On the basis of our research over recent years—including national public library and Internet surveys; focus groups with public librarians, users, and community members on uses and applications of technology in public libraries around the country; and development of statewide digital libraries and library services—we see several Internet-enabled social roles and responses now being developed and provided by the public library community. Figure 5 is a summary of some of the most important of them.

A recent Pew Internet and American Life Project report (Estabrook, Witt, and Rainie 2007) documents a broad range of Internet-enabled services currently being provided by public libraries or with significant potential to be provided by public libraries. Some of the findings from that study include the following:

Place for Public Access to the Internet. All community residents have the opportunity to come to the library and access and use the array of services and resources available on the Internet. For a majority of communities, the public library is the only place where free access to the Internet is available. This service response requires staff who are trained in assisting users locate the services/resources available and requires that the library have a high-quality technology infrastructure, e.g., adequate workstations, bandwidth, and up-to-date equipment and software.

E-Government Services Provider. Community residents rely on the public library to access federal, state, and local information and to interact effectively with these government units to obtain specific services such as completing benefits forms and obtaining child support. Staff must be knowledgeable about the range of federal, state, and local e-government services available and being requested, they must be able to assist the user in completing these forms, and they must be able to help users obtain additional information from the agencies as needed.

Emergency and Disaster Relief Provider. In times of local community emergencies, e.g., hurricanes, tornadoes, terrorist attacks, the public library is a source of current information and a means for residents to communicate with other local residents and people outside their community. Public library staff are trained to assist both residents and emergency/disaster relief staff in accessing, managing, and providing current information. Internet-enabled resources and computing technology provide the basis for the provision of these services.

Internet and Technology Trainer. Community residents rely on the public library to learn how to access and use the Internet, how to use various software applications to solve individual needs, how to use new information technologies, and how to use Internet services (e.g., e-mail). These services include one-on-one assistance that teaches users how to complete job applications and government forms and to access and understand, e.g., medical information. Library staff are both knowledgeable about these technologies and applications and high-quality trainers. The library has training facilities such that instruction can be easily and effectively provided.

Youth Educational Support Provider. Increasingly, the public library provides a broad range of support to youth in need of assistance in accessing electronic information for formal education and homeschooling educational needs. Indeed, many public libraries have specific Internet-enabled programs that are intended primarily to help youths (and parents) be successful in their educational efforts. Staff must be knowledgeable about these sources, be able to assist youths in their use, and have the skills to work with youths and young adults to apply this information to specific assignments and other projects. The library must have physical facilities that support these applications and access to these applications.

Connector of Friends, Families, and Others. An important service response of public libraries in the networked environment is serving as a means for individuals to stay in touch via e-mail and other applications with friends, family, and other individuals. Tourists use the public library to contact children and friends; in natural disasters, people use the public library to track their family members and friends; immigrants stay in touch with families back home (wherever that is); and a range of

Figure 5 Selected Internet-enabled service roles and responses

business and other communication is conducted electronically at the library. To meet this service response, the library must have an adequate number of public-access workstations to meet user demand throughout the day and staff who can assist those who need basic training to access various communication services.

Anyplace Anywhere Anytime Individualized Information Provider. Local residents and others can now access services such as Ask-a-Librarian electronically through e-mail, chat, handheld devices, and in some instances video streaming and blogs. Significantly, users can access such service anyplace, anytime, and from virtually anywhere. Librarians must be trained to use interactive Internet-enabled communication software, develop etiquette skills, and use a range of electronic resource-sharing approaches to make this information available.

Digital Library Manager. For many users of public libraries, the primary access and use of the library is through the library's digital website. Indeed, many of the library's services and resources are easier to access and use electronically than in person. The construction of a public library's virtual digital library via the Web is significantly different than the provision of services and resources in a physical facility. To be successful in this service response, the library staff must have knowledge of the design and management of digital libraries, determine how best to provide electronic resources to its virtual users, and have a modern and high-quality technology information infrastructure platform for the digital library.

Virtual, Seamless, and Endless Electronic Resources Provider. Residents may not know where a resource is located, who owns it, or how it can be quickly obtained. They only know that they need the item *now*. Public libraries respond by having statewide and nationally developed electronic resource-sharing networks that are virtual, seamless, extensive, and almost instantaneous in the provision of these resources— often in full text. The public library must participate in such networks, understand how to make these resources available "just-in-time," and have the technology infrastructure and bandwidth for such resources to be delivered directly to the user.

Digital Workplace/space. The public library provides digital tools, resources, and services that residents can use whenever they wish (from the library or remotely). These tools may include blogs, wikis, digital cameras, RSS feeds, threaded discussion lists, and more. Access to this workplace and workspace allows residents to use and experiment with current technologies to which they might not otherwise have access. Being a digital workplace/space requires the library to have state-of-the-art information technology and support as well as extremely knowledgeable staff who can work with residents on these various applications.

Digital Ombudsperson. Public librarians may go well beyond making Internet resources and services available to their users and training them on the use of these resources and services. In this service response, the librarian provides advice and specific techniques for applying and integrating various digital and Internet-enabled services and resources to meet specific needs of the user. Once again, providing a digital ombudsperson service response requires the library to have state-of-the-art information technology and support as well as extremely knowledgeable staff who can work with residents on creative and innovative solutions in various digital applications.

Figure 5   Selected Internet-enabled service roles and responses (cont.)

- The Internet is a go-to source. In general, more people turn to the Internet (at home, work, libraries, or other places) than to any other source of information and support, including experts and family members.
- Libraries meet special needs. Young adults in Generation Y (age 18–29) are the heaviest users of libraries when they face problems.
- 65% of adults who went to a library for problem-solving help said that access to computers, particularly the Internet, was a key reason they chose the library.

This study targeted the important role of libraries in providing access to government information and e-government, but it also identified many Internet-enabled service roles and responses beyond those described in figure 5.

Additional Internet-enabled roles and responses may be *proposed* beyond those in figure 5, but those listed are the ones we have identified or have seen demonstrated on a consistent basis. Taken together, these roles currently in use in many public libraries suggest a significant change in the roles libraries promote and the expectations and needs they attempt to meet for particular communities. Some aspects of these Internet-enabled social roles as compared to traditional service roles include the following:

Attention to local communities and virtual communities. Public libraries must consider services that are used locally as well as those that are used remotely. Thus, the development and administration of these services are significantly different than depicted in the traditional service roles.

Measurement. Evaluation of the success or impact of providing these social roles has become extremely complex. Measures that once were thought to be straightforward, such as online database searches, are difficult at best to compute.

Expanding and changing technology skills and knowledge. Although some might argue that librarians have always had to change and adapt to new technologies, others can argue that the skills and knowledge librarians have had to learn and update are a magnitude larger in scale than those prior to the Internet.

Costs. The expectations of society for public libraries to be a technology service center (however defined) require a range of resources in terms of staff, budget, and equipment. These costs have to be updated on a regular basis, contributing to overall costs that were not part of the public library's budget when meeting traditional service roles.

Consortium models for services delivery. Resource sharing is a term that has been employed in the provision of public library services for years. Resource sharing (national, regional, and local) and consortium administration/delivery of Internet-enabled services have significantly complicated public library service roles.

Anyplace and anytime delivery of resources and services. Internet-enabled services allow for what have been dubbed "just-in-time" information resources and services. The physical location of the resource or service has little importance, whereas in traditional public library services the physical place for provision of that resource or service mattered a great deal to the user.

Information policies. Public libraries have always had to be concerned with federal, state, and local information policies, but this arena has expanded considerably with the arrival of Internet-enabled service roles. The various technology, telecommunications, national security, privacy, and other policy issues in the Internet environment are significantly different and often more complex than with the traditional service roles.

These are some of the factors that can be considered in recognizing the move from traditional service roles to Internet-enabled service roles. In short, the move of public libraries to Internet-enabled service roles has numerous implications for defining public libraries and their role in society.

IMPLICATIONS FOR MANAGEMENT, PLANNING, AND EVALUATION

The findings discussed above suggest that the social and service roles of public libraries have changed and continue to change as a result of the focus public librarians give to the provision of Internet access and related technology services. The data also make clear that public libraries are not necessarily tying their activities related to the Internet to the established social roles of the marketplace of ideas. The focus has shifted away from the set of clear social roles to more attention on providing Internet access and supporting a range of related technologies. But the central question is whether the provision of Internet access is a social role in and of itself or a support mechanism to facilitate other service roles. Instead of finding ways to best use the new technologies to support their traditional social roles, public libraries seem to be reducing those roles and increasing the provision of Internet-enabled services, as shown in figure 5.

An interesting implication of this situation may be that public libraries have lessened their attention to the established social roles without having a particular vision for new social roles more in tune with today's Internet-focused and technology-based society. With nearly 100% of libraries now connected to the Internet, it is quite sensible to consider the meaning and impact of near universal connectivity for public libraries in society. There is a considerable difference between focusing on children's story hour as part of the established social roles of a formal education support center and preschoolers' door to learning and focusing on the number of terminals available in the children's section.

When public libraries made the shift from an arbiter of public taste to a marketplace of ideas, the change was deliberate and widely discussed, and it resulted in changes in planning and advocacy strategies. Beyond the common belief that more technology is better, there does not seem to be a similar reasoned and planned vision for the social roles of public libraries as providers of

Internet access and services. Public librarians have yet to think through their social roles and resultant service roles in the networked society, especially how to merge, augment, or change their traditional social roles with their new role as provider of Internet access and services.

If public libraries fail to reconcile their established roles with the new Internet-enabled service roles, they risk losing track of their established roles and failing to define new ones. Several issues could result if traditional roles are not taken seriously in the rush to meet the new Internet-enabled service roles (as outlined in figure 5). In fact, there is evidence that some of these problem areas are already becoming manifest.

First, it may become difficult for public libraries to seek community support on the local level if their social roles in the community are too closely tied to technology. Within a community, free public Internet may currently or sometime in the future also be available from public elementary and secondary schools, local or state government offices, colleges, various community technology centers, bookstores, coffeehouses, or even local community wireless networks. If the social roles of public libraries in communities are too dominated by Internet access, it may be difficult for communities to remember the other reasons public libraries are important and the established social roles they have so long fulfilled. This possibility seems to be heightened by the fact that public libraries are not generally reaching out to local businesses, community organizations, and governments with the Internet services and training.

Second, the emphasis on the role of technology provider over the established roles may also create problems at the national level in terms of public policy. Being perceived by the federal government as merely a network of providers of free Internet access significantly increases the likelihood that the federal government will fail to support adequately the range of Internet-enabled services they provide. A marketplace of ideas seems less likely to be pliable in the eyes of the federal government than a network of Internet access providers. This change in perception by the federal government may already have begun, as suggested by the spate of recent legislation, including CIPA, the USA PATRIOT Act, and the Homeland Security Act, which created new restrictions of information use in libraries and established new means by which the government can collect information in public libraries (Jaeger and Burnett 2005; Jaeger et al. 2004). These restrictions run contrary to the social roles of the marketplace of ideas but seem more in line with controlling libraries like a network. Further evidence of the federal government perception of control of libraries through the control of Internet access can be found in the temporary suspension of E-rate funds in 2004, which forced some libraries into budget crises (Jaeger, McClure, and Bertot 2005; Jaeger et al. 2005). Simply put, the autonomy of the library may be eroding as the federal government more closely links public libraries not to established social roles but to providing Internet access.

Third, and perhaps most significant, moving too far from the established social roles related to the marketplace of ideas may alter the meaning of the profession. The established social roles of libraries are inextricably tied to the notion that librarianship is a socially conscious and proactive profession. The

Library Bill of Rights, which formalized the process of public libraries being marketplaces of ideas, led directly to the established social roles. The shift to the marketplace of ideas directly reflected the decision of the profession to embrace a socially active, socially conscious role in the community (Berning-hausen 1953; Fiske 1959; Gellar 1974, 1984; Robbin 1996; Stielow 2001). Loosening focus on the established social roles related to the marketplace of ideas risks the loss of the soul of librarianship—active dedication to helping the community in numerous ways. With sufficient focus, the Internet-enabled library can clearly use technology to enhance its role as the marketplace of ideas. However, if the technology access role subsumes the established social roles, many of the socially conscious and socially active dimensions may fade as monitoring, maintaining, and upgrading technology become primary activities of the profession.

Finally, as a matter of practical concern, public librarians have yet to inte-grate successfully service planning with technology planning; buying and installing technology do not necessarily support service roles. By the early 1990s, McClure (1993) was critical of continuing to use the 1987 *Planning and Role Setting for Public Libraries* since it did not integrate technology planning into services planning. Despite such concerns, the PLA planning manual efforts in 1999 and 2001 did not integrate technology and services planning. Indeed, the recent PLA technology planning manual for public libraries, *Technology for Results,* is still a technology planning manual (Mayo 2005). Although it does reference the thirteen service roles in *The New Planning for Results* manual of 2001 (Nelson 2001) and has "Developing Service-Based Plans" as a subtitle, the PLA has not successfully integrated services and technology planning on a practical, how-to-do-it basis. This situation is but another indicator of technol-ogy planning (including Internet access) as a primary driver of public library planning—with inadequate attention to linking traditional public library social Internet-enabled roles and the networked environment.

A key theme of this chapter is the implications of the public library moving from the social role of a marketplace of ideas to a provider of Internet access and services. The 2007 service responses list "Connect to the Online World" as one possible service response. Connecting (providing access) is not the same as providing Internet-enabled service roles as outlined in figure 5—many of which can be done well only by a public library. In short, the public library cannot simply be a connector or provide access to the Internet. It must marry Internet-enabled service roles into larger social roles such that its importance is increased in the networked environment.

8

Community Needs, Service Roles, and Planning

Meeting the community's information and other needs, especially in the Internet environment, is an important planning component for public libraries. Typically a community has an identity—that is, people see themselves as part of a particular community (Putnam 1999). Moreover, members of a community may have shared beliefs, values, and goals. Traditionally, communities have been geographically based, although increasingly online or virtual communities continue to develop and evolve. How the needs of these communities are translated into public library planning and service roles and responses poses several issues.

IDENTIFYING INTERNET-ENABLED SERVICE NEEDS

Although notions of community similarity may be true at a macro level, on a day-to-day basis librarians encounter and serve many different groups of individuals within one community. Indeed, the degree to which public libraries can successfully meet service role expectations of all groups within the community is often problematic. From a historical perspective, meeting community-based Internet information needs since roughly the mid-1990s has seen a substantial shift in service orientation in a relatively limited amount of time.

The significant demands from community groups to obtain Internet-enabled services and resources from the public library can come at the expense of other traditional library service roles. Given the significant costs of purchasing and deploying a technology infrastructure to support Internet-enabled services and the stagnant or limited growth in many public library budgets, a significant shift may be occurring in which public libraries are moving to better meet the needs of one group in the local community—those demanding more and better Internet-enabled services—at the expense of other community information needs represented by traditional service roles.

One reflection of this change is evident in how public libraries define their community and its needs and which services they provide to which groups. This process may be under revision, and it may require considerable revision. The move toward meeting Internet-enabled information service demands may be occurring by default, without adequate consideration of the impacts resulting from this change—for example, reduced or eliminated traditional information services and resources in other library service areas or failure to integrate traditional and Internet-enabled roles adequately.

From the research reported here and our observations regarding the Internet-enabled services as shown in figure 5, there does not appear to be a conscious and well-defined effort on the part of librarians to identify community computing needs, develop service roles to meet those needs, and implement and administer the activities related to these roles. Although there are clearly a variety of community-based computing and Internet needs, the response appears to be less one of conscious planning (as described in Nelson 2008) and more one of simply having more workstations, more bandwidth, more databases to search, and more Internet-enabled applications (e.g., Ask-a-Librarian) for the community.

PRESCRIPTIVE VERSUS DESCRIPTIVE SERVICE ROLES

An issue that continues to be debated is the degree to which public library service roles are descriptive—based on what the public library community actually does—or prescriptive, based on what the library thinks the community, and thus the library, *should* do. To a large extent, the service roles introduced in 1987 and modified and updated through 2007 have remained largely descriptive, that is, they describe a menu of rather standard and typical service activities from which public libraries can choose those most suited to their particular community.

This issue is similar to the collection development issue of "give 'em what they want versus give 'em what they need." In the instance of developing Internet-enabled service roles, however, both communities and librarians may not know enough about possible roles to know what is possible or what is needed. Thus, without a list of service roles that are imaginative and forward-thinking, public library Internet service roles may not evolve as quickly as Internet applications in other parts of society.

For example, if the Internet service roles suggested in figure 5 were widely circulated, would they serve as a catalyst for additional public libraries to move into the provision of these types of services? Since some public libraries may have limited familiarity with the Internet service roles, an awareness that these service roles are possible may encourage the public library to experiment with them. But since these roles are more prescriptive than descriptive—and not included in the 2007 service roles—public libraries may not recognize the range of opportunities available.

The notion of public library planning based on incorporating predetermined service roles and responses (whether traditional or Internet-enabled) has a taste of arrogance inasmuch as they are intended to be useful for all types of libraries in all types of settings. Simon notes:

> As I have talked with thousands of individuals about their libraries, I have been struck by the number of ways in which [a library] is defined. . . . The PLA service responses tend to focus on the informational service of the library rather than a variety of other public benefits that may have little to do with the library's information sources. (2002, 104)

Simon goes on to outline service roles and responses that are especially important for his library but are not among the (then) thirteen PLA service responses, and he concludes that planning based on predetermined service responses can result in the undesirable attitude of "Pick a service response . . . any response as long as it comes from the professionally approved list."

Public library planning is a process to help the library better identify and meet the needs of its communities. But the service responses that best fit the needs of the community may not be any of those listed in previous attempts to articulate roles and responses. Moreover, those service responses may have little relationship to broader social roles of public libraries. Planning is a process that should assist librarians and community members to identify opportunities for the public library to fulfill needs that might not be addressed by others in the community or in society. Reliance on traditional, descriptive public library service roles that have changed little over the past twenty years may, in fact, be a force that mitigates against change and successful service provision in the Internet environment.

SHIFT FROM TRADITIONAL TO INTERNET-ENABLED SERVICE ROLES

The degree to which public libraries have shifted to Internet-enabled service roles such as those identified in figure 5 from the provision of more traditional service roles as described in the 2008 manual (Nelson 2008) and summarized in figure 3 appears to be growing. In several data collection efforts, many public librarians easily recognized the Internet-enabled service roles in figure 5 as responses to community computing and Internet services that public librarians currently provide. In fact, as this book is being written in 2008, finding public libraries that do not provide at least one or two of these Internet-enabled service roles would be difficult.

Since public libraries now provide some or many of the Internet-enabled service roles identified in figure 5, one has to ask to what extent are the traditional service roles—those still listed in the 2007 list of service responses (Garcia and Nelson 2007)—actually being provided? And though the traditional service roles may still be provided, the *extent* to which they can be provided in 2008 has had to change significantly since 1987. Most libraries have not had significant increases in budgets, staff, and other resources such that a range of new and expensive Internet-enabled services can be continuously added to library services without limiting other service roles.

Have the traditional service roles, begun in 1987, outlived their usefulness? Have Internet-enabled service roles supplanted these traditional roles, resulting in a monumental change in the nature of public library social roles? Or are the Internet-enabled social roles less a set of service roles and more a set of activities—not related to larger social roles—that public libraries now provide to meet the needs and expectations of their communities? Although the truth may be somewhere in between, we would argue that the shift to Internet-enabled service roles and responses has, in fact, had a significant effect on societal expectations of the public library and the manner in which a public library is now defined. It is not that the traditional service responses are inappropriate or unused; it is a matter of degree and emphasis by which they have been reduced by the inclusion and growth of Internet-enabled service roles. Of equal importance, however, is the possibility that public library planning—including the integration of technology and services planning—simply has not kept pace with the development of public library Internet-enabled service roles.

Planning for Service Roles and Planning for Technology

The link between selected PLA service roles and responses and technology planning continues to be problematic for public librarians. As early as 1993, McClure, Ryan, and Moen noted:

> Another serious limitation of *Planning and Role Setting for Public Libraries* is its inattention to technology planning in general, and planning for the networked environment in particular. There is discontinuity in the manual between planning for service and planning the technology infrastructure needed to support those services. . . . The manual needs to be revised to link technology planning with services planning and to encourage public library planners to plan for technology development and implementation as well as services. (1993, 26)

Little progress in linking these two activities has been made since this criticism was expressed. Typically public libraries do not have a formal technology plan, and if they have one it has little integration with the PLA library service roles.

PLA public library technology planning manuals (Mayo and Nelson 1999; Mayo 2005) as well as other technology planning guides (e.g., Cohen, Kelsey, and Fiels 2001; Courtney 2005) discuss the importance of public library service roles either not at all or only in passing. For example, the PLA argues that, "although it is possible to develop a technology plan without a service plan, it is not recommended" (Mayo 2005, 2) and goes on to suggest that, if service responses have not been selected, such selection should occur prior to developing the technology plan. In addition, the PLA materials suggest:

> A technology plan is a plan for acquiring and expanding technology-related resources. It is about filling the gap between what you have available to achieve your service objectives and what you determine you need to achieve those objectives. To do this you need:
>
> - an inventory of the elements of your current technology infrastructure; and
> - projections of the technology infrastructure you will require to support planned services of improved productivity.
>
> The difference between what you have and what you need is what you plan to do. (Mayo 2005, 7)

At issue is the use of the term *service objectives* and the degree to which these objectives are similar to or different from service roles and responses.

The 2007 service responses do provide some information about the technology that is associated with a particular service response. For example, for the service response "Gets Facts Fast," the technology resources needed are telephone call queuing software, chat software, and text messaging software (Nelson 2008, 178). Although these are certainly needed, they cannot begin to address the technology infrastructure required to provide real-time digital reference services. Thus, if this service response is selected and is planned to be provided via an Internet-enabled approach, implementing it without a better understanding of the current information technology infrastructure in the library and the degree to which it can support the service response is likely to be problematic.

Our experience with both public library service plans and technology plans is that there tends to be more talk about having such plans than there is actually having and using such plans. The level of effort required to develop a useful service plan and technology plan—to say nothing of a service plan and technology plan that are integrated and coordinated—is significant. Clearly, public libraries are now at a point at which services planning cannot be done successfully without integrating that plan into technology planning. There is a need to develop *one* planning approach that in *one* process integrates services planning with technology planning.

A key issue for public library planners in the Internet-enabled service environment, then, is how best to integrate services planning as outlined in the 2008 manual (Nelson 2008) with technology planning as outlined in the 2005 manual (Mayo 2005). The 1987 manual (McClure et al. 1987) did not operate in the Internet-enabled environment, but the 2001 and 2008 service planning manuals and service responses do operate in this environment (Nelson 2001, 2008). One simply cannot select service roles in 2008 without carefully considering the information technology infrastructure needed to support those roles—regardless of whether they are the service responses listed in the 2008 manual or the service roles identified by us and listed in figure 5.

PLANNING FOR INTERNET-ENABLED SERVICE ROLES

The ability of public libraries to fulfill Internet-enabled service roles may be declining. There have been signs for several years that libraries are struggling to meet demands as a result of a combination of factors, such as the limits on physical space in libraries, the increasing complexity of Internet content, the continual costs of Internet access and computer maintenance, the inherent limitations of the telecommunications grid, and the rising demands for bandwidth, processing speed, and number of workstations (Bertot, McClure, and Jaeger 2005; Jaeger, Bertot, and McClure 2007; Jaeger et al. 2006; Jaeger, Bertot, et al. 2007; Jaeger and Fleischmann 2007).

The 2007 *Public Library and the Internet* survey data indicate that many libraries have hit an infrastructure plateau for provision of and access to Internet services. These constraints are now preventing libraries from increasing connection speeds, numbers of workstations, processing capacities, and services; in many cases, the infrastructure plateau relates directly to insufficient funding, physical space, and staffing to meet the Internet access expectations of patrons, communities, and governments (McClure, Jaeger, and Bertot 2007). This plateau comes precisely at a time when community demand for more and better Internet-enabled services appears to be expanding.

Thus, a contradiction is developing between the expectations for free public library Internet access services and what libraries can actually provide. Data from the 2007 survey, and previous surveys, indicate that many libraries are having trouble meeting the Internet access needs of their patrons and communities. Indeed, in the 2007 survey only 22% of respondents reported that there were sufficient public Internet workstations available to patrons throughout the day. This situation raises the issue of how much longer libraries will be able to maintain a range of growing Internet-enabled service roles without failing to meet traditional and other community expectations.

We may, then, need a reconsideration of the degree to which public libraries can provide which service roles (traditional, Internet-enabled, or both) and to which members of their community and, collectively, to society. Although there may be limited recognition that local public library service roles shape the perceptions and expectations of society regarding public library social roles, such is likely the case. For example, our research related to e-government and public libraries clearly demonstrated that state and federal government officials expect public libraries to provide a range of e-government services and have, in fact, notified residents that they should go to the public library to access and obtain professional assistance with these services (see chapter 6).

9

Selecting Internet-Enabled Service Roles

Although the process for selecting Internet-enabled service roles is similar to the process for selecting traditional service roles, additional factors should be considered. Even though the Internet is now an essential aspect of many roles of public libraries, the technical dimensions require specific considerations. Internet-enabled service roles require the library staff and planning committee to become familiar with the various possible Internet-enabled service roles, assess the degree to which the library has the technological infrastructure to support these roles, determine their appropriateness for the particular community, and then determine how best to implement and evaluate the library's success in providing these services.

The summary of possible Internet-enabled service roles shown in figure 5 is illustrative only, and there are likely to be additional such service roles appropriate for each library community. Given an individual library's experiences in the provision of Internet-enabled services, there is likely to be a need to refine and further specify the service roles in figure 5 or create entirely new service roles. The outline of factors that can be used to describe a service role as employed in Garcia and Nelson (2007) is a good beginning point when developing new Internet-enabled service roles. Figure 5 is a good starting place to gain a better understanding of the nature and type of resources needed to support these roles.

As an example, if a library wants to provide the role "Connector of Friends, Families, and Others," it needs to

- assist users in establishing and operating various free e-mail services, blogs, wikis, threaded discussion lists, and the like
- train users in basic commands and procedures for these communication services and be able to assist them in locating e-mail and other types of addresses to communicate with others
- provide adequate numbers of high-quality workstations for users to engage in the range of communication services
- offer physical facilities where users can access computer workstations in a comfortable manner and with some privacy
- make available knowledgeable staff who can work, typically, one on one with users
- provide adequate bandwidth to support these communication services as well as other library networked services

Depending on a library's local community, there may be other issues to consider, such as the need for staff to have foreign language skills. The staff may need to review a variety of resources related to a particular Internet-enabled service role in order to follow up on the implications and impacts of providing that role. In short, library staff and members of the planning committee must recognize the implications of providing a specific service role and the degree to which staff will be knowledgeable enough about the role to implement it successfully.

Our experience is that an assessment of the current quality and sufficiency of the library's information technology infrastructure and telecommunications bandwidth is an important next step in the process of selecting Internet-enabled service roles (Bertot and McClure 2007). There is little point in determining the need for or appropriateness of a particular Internet-enabled service role without knowledge of the adequacy of the technology infrastructure and bandwidth. Knowledge of the library's technology infrastructure and sufficiency of bandwidth informs the process of selecting Internet-enabled service roles and determining what steps might have to be taken to expand that infrastructure if a particular service role is to be provided.

For purposes of this discussion, the library's technology infrastructure is the collection of workstations, databases, vendor services, computing and telecommunications hardware and software, network configurations, and knowledge and skills of those individuals responsible for operating this infrastructure. A complete self-assessment of a library's technology infrastructure is beyond the scope of this book. Figure 6, however, is a general overview of the process by which library staff can better understand the basic quality and sufficiency of their technology infrastructure.

A first step is to inventory and describe the current library infrastructure, network, and Internet-enabled service roles currently being provided. Items such as the following should be identified and described:

- number of workstations (public and administrative) operated in the library

- availability of wireless networks in the library
- bandwidth coming into the library and actual bandwidth available at individual workstations
- number and skills of technology support staff; network configuration, that is, how the various computers and networked services are linked and organized

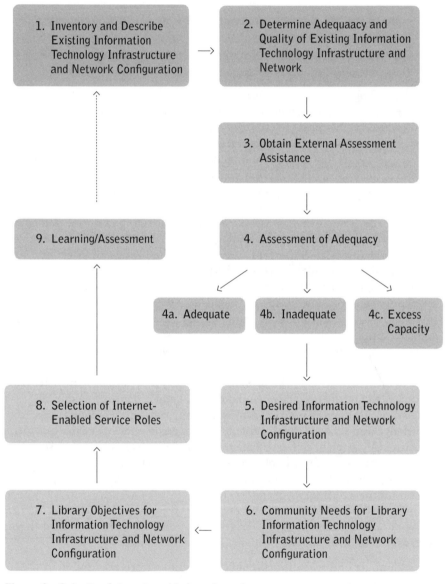

Figure 6   Selecting Internet-enabled service roles

- physical facilities that support computing and public-access workstations
- networked databases and other services provided by the library
- specific types of Internet-enabled service roles being provided (see figure 5 and add others)
- types of uses patrons make of the public-access workstations, such as e-mail, file sharing, streaming video

A revealing exercise is to test the actual speed of workstation connectivity (bandwidth) by using a test site such as www.speakeasy.net/speedtest/. Test the availability of bandwidth through this website for different workstations at different times to determine the bandwidths available and how they fluctuate throughout the day. Step one should result in a brief report that addresses the above topics and provides a diagram of the network connectivity and configuration of items supported by the network.

Library staff can refer to descriptive data for their library and computer services from *Libraries Connect Communities: Public Library Funding and Technology Access Study* (American Library Association and Information Institute 2007), the *Public Library Data Service Statistical Report* (Public Library Association 2007), and data provided to TechAtlas on WebJunction (www.webjunction.org/do/Home) to assist in the description of the existing library information technology infrastructure and network configuration. Some 6,500 public libraries contributed to the 2007 Public Library Funding and Technology Access Study, so many public libraries already have this descriptive data.

A second step is to determine the degree to which the existing technology infrastructure and bandwidth are adequate and provide high-quality support for existing services. In essence, the assessment is to compare the infrastructure and bandwidth against the actual networked services and resources being provided. This step is part art and part science; some libraries obtain assistance from the state library staff or others to make this determination. The question of how much infrastructure and bandwidth are enough must be determined locally, given the situation in which the library uses that infrastructure and bandwidth. Ultimately, this assessment results in one of three possible conclusions: the existing information technology infrastructure and bandwidth are inadequate to support existing networked services and resources, are adequate to support these services and resources, or have excess capacity to provide additional networked services and resources.

It is critically important to understand the relationship between information technology capacity and use before attempting to decide the range of Internet-enabled service roles the library may wish to provide. For example, if the library has one T1 line providing connectivity for all library services, forty workstations connected to that T1 line, and also a wireless router that allows up to fifty simultaneous connections, it is possible that individuals at a particular workstation are, in effect, working with a 56 kbps connection. Adding Internet-enabled service roles in this environment will be unsuccessful unless additional bandwidth can be obtained. Indeed, if the library cannot increase the bandwidth, it might consider reducing the number of available connections to ensure that its Internet access is sufficiently useful to individual patrons.

Our experience in conducting such assessments is that some public libraries have inadequate information technology infrastructure and bandwidth to support their existing networked services and resources adequately. Of equal concern is that often the staffs of these libraries are unaware of this inadequacy and add more workstations or wireless connections without increasing bandwidth, usually resulting in a degradation of the quality of their Internet access.

A next step is to describe the information technology infrastructure, network configuration, and Internet service roles the library would like to be able to provide. These are targets and suggest possible objectives yet to be accomplished—unless the library has previously determined that it has excess capacity in its information technology infrastructure and network configuration. When detailing the preferred state for the technology infrastructure and network configuration, these questions may be useful:

- What are the Internet-enabled service roles and other types of networked services and resources that the library would like to provide?
- What specific types of computing hardware (workstations, servers, routers, cabling, etc.) and software are needed to meet these service needs and roles?
- Given the Internet-enabled service roles and other networked services that would be provided, what types of Internet connectivity and bandwidth are necessary?
- How might the network configuration be redesigned to better support the Internet-enabled service roles and other networked services and resources?
- Are there advanced Web 2.0 (or 3.0) networked services that should be provided by the library?

Several guides are available to assist library staff in determining the types of infrastructure and network needed to meet advanced Internet-enabled service roles and networked services and resources (Casey and Savastinuk 2007; Courtney 2007). Once again, this step should result in a report that summarizes the desired information technology infrastructure and network configuration.

The next steps in the selection of Internet-enabled service roles are to consider community needs for use of the library information infrastructure and its network and the library needs and objectives for information technology infrastructure and the library's network. Library staff can conduct surveys or focus group sessions with community members to assess community computing needs. Staff may also be aware of these needs through their interactions with community members both within and outside the library. But the key questions to answer are these:

- What types of computing hardware and software best meet community needs?

- What are the demographic characteristics of public-access computer users and how do they use computers?
- What is the extent of the demand for library computing and Internet-enabled services from the community?
- Are there other organizations in the community that provide free public access to computing and Internet services?
- What Internet-enabled service roles and resources are of most importance to community members?
- What connectivity speeds and bandwidth are required to support these Internet-enabled services and resources?

Depending on the nature of the local library and community, a range of other questions can be answered to describe community needs for library information infrastructure and network configuration.

Given the information that has been collected thus far, library staff should now describe their needs and objectives for library information infrastructure and network configuration. If there are considerable needs yet to be met and the objectives of the library's information technology infrastructure and network configuration require considerable time and resources to accomplish, then the current extent of Internet-enabled service roles that can be provided with acceptable quality may be modest.

These Internet-enabled service roles could be expanded when the library is able to expand its information technology infrastructure and network. On the other hand, the library may find that it can expand its Internet-enabled service roles because it has excess capacity and the infrastructure supports community computing and Internet services needs. Either way, the provision of Internet-enabled service roles must be supported by adequate library information technology infrastructure and network support.

In light of the information the library has collected from the above activities, discussions about which Internet-enabled service roles are most appropriate and can be adequately supported can take place both within the library and with the board of trustees or library planning committee. When selecting these service roles, the library may also wish to consider the following:

- Generally, it is better to select fewer Internet-enabled service roles and do them well than to select too many roles and do them poorly.
- The Internet-enabled service roles should be carefully coordinated with the traditional service roles the library provides.
- Measures and strategies to evaluate the Internet-enabled service roles should be developed and implemented.
- Some Internet-enabled service roles require the presence of specially trained staff if the service role is to be successful.
- Some Internet-enabled service roles require regular upgrades of equipment and training.
- Important local and state political factors may affect the appropriateness of various service roles.

The final part of this Internet-enabled service role selection effort is a learning and assessment process. Within the library, staff need to determine the overall success, impact, quality, and usefulness of the Internet-enabled service roles they have implemented. Community input is needed to inform this assessment. Based on this process, both the library and the community can plan for the selection of the next set of Internet-enabled service roles.

The key points of this chapter are that the library should consciously select Internet-enabled service roles as part of the planning process and do the proper research to ensure that it can adequately support those roles given its current or readily attainable information technology infrastructure and network configuration.

10

The Future of Internet-Enabled Service Roles

The potential uses and applications of the Web in many contexts have yet to be well understood, but nevertheless they are developing rapidly. The means by which public libraries select and develop Internet-enabled service roles are also developing rapidly. It is not inconceivable, given the current speed of technological change, that the Internet-enabled service roles suggested in figure 5 may be out of date soon after the publication of this book and require wholesale changes on a regular basis. Indeed, the notion of PLA-sponsored service roles—and perhaps even Internet-enabled service roles—may itself be outdated.

The current trend in the use of social networking applications is likely to have significant impacts on Internet-enabled service roles. A recent report from OCLC notes:

> Social sites like MySpace, Mixi, Facebook and YouTube have built a new "social web" connecting communities of hundreds of millions of users across much of the industrialized world. In June 2007, the world's top three social sites (YouTube, MySpace, Facebook) attracted more than 350 million people to their Web sites according to comScore. . . . We know relatively little about what these emerging social Web communities will mean for the future of the Internet or the possibilities they hold for library services on the Internet. (OCLC 2007, vii–viii)

In the future, then, is it possible that public library users will develop their own Internet-enabled service roles that parallel or replicate library services?

Will public library Internet-enabled service roles be able to compete with user-designed socially networked and participatory services?

As only one example, the website Library Thing (www.librarything.com) provides a means for users to enter and catalog their personal library or a reading list, connects users to other people reading the same or similar books, offers recommendations of books of interest, gives blogging space, and much more. As of February 2008, members have cataloged some 23 million books. Other examples of these new types of Internet "library" service roles include Bibliocommons (www.bibliocommons.com), which is "transforming online library catalogues from searchable inventory systems into engaging social discovery environments." The notions of social networked communal cataloging, resource discovery among information and people, participatory readers' advisory, and the like have significant implications for how public library Internet-enabled service roles may evolve—or ultimately be replaced by user-developed roles that replicate library functions.

In a recent paper, Lankes, Silverstein, and Nicholson describe library service in terms of participatory networks in which the library is a "conversation." They go on to state:

> A core concept of Web 2.0 is that people are the content of sites; that is, a site is not populated with information for users to consume. Instead, services are provided to individual users for them to build networks of friends and other groups (professional, recreational, and so on). The content of a site, then, comprises user-provided information that attracts new members of an ever-expanding network. (2007, 19)

The issues discussed in this book raise numerous challenges to the future of public library Internet-enabled services. But of special interest to the topic being discussed here are several important questions: To what degree will these participatory network conversations include the public library or be developed by the public library? To what degree will public librarians be able to develop exciting and dynamic Internet-enabled service roles that are participatory and draw on social networking principles successfully?

At the heart of all of these various social networking applications is a peer-to-peer relationship of community members, and just how such relationships will affect public library Internet-enabled service roles is not well understood. Many of the social networking applications "push" services to users, offer links to other information—much of it directly from other peers—and ultimately allow Internet users to define and create information services that are personalized or customized to meet their specific needs. Perhaps more important, they encourage the development, content, and services to evolve according to participants' needs and creativity.

An underlying notion of these social networking applications is personal trust among participants and an appreciation of the value of receiving opinions from others (Kelton, Fleischmann, and Wallace 2008). Obtaining papers, publications, or online articles is not the same as obtaining the opinion, insights, and experiences of someone on a topic of special interest (e.g., dealing with cancer) who is trusted by the user and with whom the community of users has shared values. A major conclusion of the OCLC (2007) study *Sharing, Privacy and Trust in Our Networked World* is that users of these social sites increasingly have less concern about their privacy, confidentiality, and trustworthiness. Thus, they are increasingly likely to provide the personal information, views, and experiences that shape these sites.

Evaluating public library Internet-enabled service roles that are built into a social networked environment requires consideration of several factors:

- Traditional evaluation approaches typically base assessment on an imposed or organizationally accepted set of service goals/objectives. Service roles based on social networked activities build on dynamic, personally self-driven goals/objectives that are constantly changing.

- Outcome measures (for example) that assess changes in knowledge, behavior, skills, or attitudes may be less important in social networking service roles, where learning, contacts, quality of life, and other individually based measures are more important. Moreover, individually based process measures may have greater validity for measuring user success than system-based outcomes.

- Comparing the "success" of users across various types of social networking service role applications presents numerous challenges given the situational nature of users of these applications.

- The nature and definition of "community" as it relates to the library's service population change significantly in a social networking context. Successful social networking applications rely on virtual communities that span the globe, not local, geographically or politically defined communities.

- Separating the evaluation and measurement of the technological infrastructure of the service role from the actual use of that application may be impossible. In short, to what degree are evaluators measuring the quality of the technology as opposed to the use of that technology?

- Success of an individual's use of an Internet-based socially networked service role is dependent on the skills and knowledge of the user— one person's success versus another's may have little to do with the application itself.

These are but a few of the challenges the future holds for successful evaluation of public library service roles that build on social networking applications.

Published lists of traditional public library service roles may continue to be of use for many public libraries. But Internet-enabled service roles—and especially those that incorporate social networked and participatory service roles— are much more likely to evolve rapidly, depending on a range of library factors such as staff skills, available information technology infrastructure, situational factors, and skills of individual users. Thus, the public library community must become much more informed and better able to deploy Internet applications rapidly in the development, selection, administration, and evaluation of these service roles.

Lankes, Silverstein, and Nicholson conclude that "libraries have a chance not only to improve service to their local communities, but to advance the field of participatory networks" (2007, 32). This may be true, but libraries also have a chance to *not* be effective players in the development of participatory networks, *not* develop Internet-enabled service roles that build on social networking, and *not* develop valid and reliable measures to gauge the success of their involvement in such service roles. Although participatory technologies open up new opportunities for library services (Courtney 2007), they also create new roles and expectations for libraries along with many assessment, staffing, economic, and service pressures. The future of Internet-enabled service roles is one laden with challenges—and one that will be increasingly decided by individual public librarians, the development of social networking applications, vendor products, and individual Internet users.

11

Challenges from Professional Resistance and Public Policy

Internet-related roles and expectations present public libraries with significant challenges in meeting the needs of individuals, communities, and governments. We have thus far discussed challenges in staffing, education, advocacy, space, and funding, among others. There are, however, two major challenges that merit individual discussion: the fact that Internet-enabled roles and expectations are not embraced by all members of the library community, and the fact that public policy decisions often make the provision and management of Internet services more difficult for libraries.

CHALLENGES FROM WITHIN THE PROFESSION

Although libraries have existed for millennia, they have not had a static meaning. The library is a social creation and a social agency that binds members of a community together (Shera 1970), and thus its roles have often evolved to reflect the society it serves. The meaning of the library as a place within communities has varied across cultures, nations, and times (Buschman and Leckie 2007). Libraries have served a range of societal needs throughout history, including repository, information provider, educational institution, and social advocate (Reith 1984). Similarly, the philosophies associated with librarianship and the principles of educating librarians have evolved over time (McChesney 1984; Rogers 1984). Clearly, libraries have been adaptive and changing organizations.

Technology is a significant part of the changing nature of libraries. From the time public libraries began to organize around professional associations and develop professional standards in the late 1800s, technology has been important in shaping libraries and the profession of librarianship. Melvil Dewey in particular was keenly focused on the creation and novel employment of technology to improve library operations (Garrison 1993; Wiegand 1996). As new means of electronic dissemination of information—such as radio, movies, and television—became widely used, libraries reacted by eventually incorporating many of these developments into the services and types of materials they provided (McCrossen 2006; Pittman 2001; Preer 2006). By the 1960s, Jesse Shera (1964) foresaw that information technology could greatly reduce manual tasks performed by librarians. The progression of modern information technology has been a major influence on what libraries have tried to provide to their patrons and what patrons have in turn expected from their libraries.

In 1967, Shera asserted that technological evolution "will have tremendous importance for services which the library can offer, the ways in which it can offer these services, the advances it can make in its own technology, and in the whole underlying theory of what librarianship is" (1970, 70). The specific changes eventually brought by the Internet, however, proved hard for librarians to foresee. For example, the White House Conference on Library and Information Services of 1979 anticipated the time when technology would simultaneously reduce the costs of running a library and expand the services available (Seymour 1980). Though the panel predicted major changes in library services as a result of advances in information technology, their cost predictions were far from correct. In a collection of essays (Lancaster 1993) written by librarians in 1993 envisioning the library of the twenty-first century, no mention was made of the Internet or the World Wide Web as part of the library's future, though CD-ROMs received considerable attention.

Even since the Internet has become commonplace in libraries, its true impact has been downplayed or underestimated in many quarters. In 2001 many librarians viewed the Internet as primarily a basic reference tool that also had entertainment and communication capacities (Shuman 2001). In 2002 one book on the profession of librarianship helpfully noted that computer skills were probably required for any library position, though it also acknowledged that, "for library and information center staffers at all levels, the Internet has brought fundamental change to 'business as usual'" (Fourie and Dowell 2002, 254).

Some have also suggested that certain aspects of the Internet and related technologies run contrary to or undermine the established social roles of public libraries as a marketplace of ideas. Critics—both in the popular media and within libraries—have attacked libraries' perceived confusion of purpose and rush toward the Internet, which is seen as entertainment, and away from books, which are viewed as the substance of a more pure service to communities (Baker 1996, 2001; Tisdale 1997). Others (e.g., Brown and Duguid 2002; Buschman 2003) have raised these issues:

- New technologies are expensive.
- The costs of these new technologies cut into spending on more traditional materials.

- Electronic information is not permanent.
- Much of the information provided by the Internet falls outside the parameters of information provided by other media in the library.
- Computers have no place in the library.

And these are not the most extreme views taken in reaction to rise of the Internet as a core aspect of public library services.

Some even view the Internet as a possible means of demise for libraries if the profession does not change. For example, the introduction to a recent book states that libraries are "under threat" and seem "to belong to a bygone age." The author asserts: "I fear for them," "there is a real danger that libraries and librarians will be left behind" and "could so easily become backwaters" (Brophy 2007, x). All of this because of the Internet.

Resistance to or fear of the Internet and its impacts is hardly unique to libraries, of course. The Internet reaches into virtually every dimension of a technologically advanced society. Renowned computer scientist Ben Shneiderman (2008) has even suggested that the technological revolutions of the past twenty years are so all-encompassing and significant in shaping society that traditional scientific methods need to be reconceptualized. The public library is far from alone in rethinking its meaning as a social institution. Yet this issue seems to be particularly hard for certain quarters in public libraries.

Fears related to the Internet among the library community, however they are expressed, are real and must be addressed. Some of this fear is fairly abstract. Some people are concerned that computers in libraries encourage the dissipation of authority, of history, and of continuity through a "technocracy" that replaces the traditional purpose of libraries (Buschman 2003). Other fears are rooted in perception: the increasing appearance of computers in libraries makes libraries appear similar to many other social institutions. "At this historical moment, the changes that libraries are undergoing make them appear to be complicit with other contemporary forces that are eroding access to history and unraveling the connections of past and future generations" (Manoff 2001, 374). A further factor may be that libraries have historically been considered refuges in times of social change (Rayward and Jenkins 2007), but these social changes—in the tangible form of computers in the library buildings—reach into the essence of the library itself. "We subconsciously know that libraries are more complex than information centers" (Dowell 2008, 42). For many librarians, though, the presence of computers may make libraries seem too much like information centers only.

The hesitance to embrace or outright resistance to acknowledge the centrality of Internet-enabled library service roles is revealed in the ambivalence with which certain evaluation texts treat the technology. The 2007 PLA study of the roles of public libraries has already been discussed at length, but it is not alone. For example, in a recent book on library evaluation, the evaluation of electronic resources, technical services, and online systems are each separate chapters from traditional services such as users, the physical collection, reference services, customer service, and interlibrary loan (Matthews 2007).

Similarly, in a 2004 book on measuring library effectiveness, the same author infrequently mentions the Internet or related technologies (Matthews 2004a). This is surprising, for the book was extremely popular and well written in other aspects. By treating these topics individually rather than as integrated aspects of librarianship, these books seem not to acknowledge how central technology is to library services. This separation is even more curious when one considers that the same author has also written a book on preparing library technology plans (Matthews 2004b). If nothing else, this demonstrates the ambivalence with which many still regard the Internet and related technologies within the meaning of public libraries.

One area of agreement between proponents and critics of the Internet in public libraries is that it has shaped their social roles significantly in the past twenty years. Many of the problems faced by libraries in dealing with new technologies and information sources through the years are similar to those faced now in relation to the Internet in that they force a reconsideration of the roles the library wants to play in society (Preer 2006). As examples among countless others, the digital age has forced libraries to redefine the meaning of intellectual freedom in libraries and the meaning of the library as public forum (Dresang 2006; Gathegi 2005).

Whatever the various reasons behind the resistance to Internet-enabled roles and expectations, such views are unrealistic and unhelpful in the planning and use of Internet technology. The public library is not likely to retrograde technologically. In the past century, it has adopted and absorbed many different technologies to continue to expand its services, remain relevant to patrons, and build trust in communities (Jaeger and Fleischmann 2007; McCrossen 2006; Pittman 2001; Preer 2006). There are now clear societal expectations that public libraries must have Internet-enabled services and be able to fulfill social roles based on these technologies. At this point, these roles are defining public libraries as much if not more than traditional service roles. The sooner all segments of the library community embrace this reality, the better position libraries will be in to confront other challenges to the provision of these services, such as difficulties based in public policy decisions.

CHALLENGES FROM PUBLIC POLICY

Laws related to the technology and Internet access provided by libraries—such as the USA PATRIOT Act, CIPA, the Homeland Security Act, the E-government Act, the Telecommunications Act of 1996, and LSTA, among others—have added new constraints in information provision and access in libraries, from mandating filtering of Internet access to creating new guidelines for what electronic information can be requested from libraries in investigations (Jaeger, Bertot, and McClure 2004; Jaeger and Burnett 2005; Jaeger et al. 2006). All of these laws influence how the library serves its role as marketplace of ideas through use of electronic resources. The following are just a brief sample of challenges presented to public libraries by information policy.

TELECOMMUNICATIONS

The success with which public libraries can participate effectively in providing Internet access and resources is related to the quality and sufficiency of the bandwidth available in the library (Bertot and McClure 2007). Overall, the policy and technological environments surrounding broadband are extremely complicated in the United States (Weiser 2008). In recent years, there have been significant disputes about the U.S. broadband policy environment and the degree to which federal telecommunications and broadband policy does (National Telecommunications and Information Administration 2008) or does not (Center for Creative Voices in Media 2007) promote increased access to broadband with higher quality and reduced cost.

Findings from various studies suggest that public libraries that have reduced broadband access also have limitations on the range of Internet-enabled services and resources they can provide (American Library Association and Information Institute 2007). Such is especially true in the provision of large data sources such as those available from the National Aeronautics and Space Administration (www.nasa.gov) or many of the Web 2.0 technologies that require large amounts of bandwidth for video, audio, interactive, and other social networking capacities. There are several broadband information policy issues related to access, quality, cost, and availability (rural vs. urban areas) that affect the success with which public libraries can engage in meeting expectations for Internet-enabled services.

E-RATE AND UNIVERSAL SERVICE

Within the broad topic of telecommunications policy is the information policy issue of E-rate and universal service, which affects the quality and sufficiency of public library provision of Internet access. The Telecommunications Act of 1996 established a Universal Service Fund administered by the Universal Service Administrative Company to oversee the Schools and Libraries Program (www.usac.org/about/universal-service/). As part of this program, public libraries can apply for E-rate support to obtain discounts for selected telecommunications, Internet access, and internal connectivity. These discounts are sizable, ranging from 20% to 90%. The procedures for requesting these discounts have been criticized for a range of reasons (Jaeger, Bertot, et al. 2007; Jaeger, McClure, and Bertot 2005). Libraries receive only 4% of total E-rate funds, yet this amount is quite substantial, with public libraries receiving more than $250 million between 2000 and 2003 (Jaeger, McClure, and Bertot 2005).

The American Library Association (2002) has noted that the E-rate program has been particularly significant in its role of expanding online access to library patrons in both rural and underserved communities. In addition to the impact on libraries, E-rate and LSTA funds have affected the lives of individuals and communities in a significant way. Goldstein (2002) has estimated that approximately 11 million low-income individuals rely on public libraries to access online information. Ultimately, the success with which a public library can work through the E-rate application procedures has a direct bearing on the quality of the library's information infrastructure and degree to which that infrastructure can support provision of Internet-enabled services.

HOMELAND SECURITY

The degree to which public libraries can successfully deliver the full range of government information and services that they are expected to provide has been aggravated by national security policies that resulted from the terrorist attacks of September 11, 2001. Since the attacks, federal, state, and local government information has been much more carefully scrutinized for perceived national security information to ensure that such information is not released to the public. The tighter controls over access to public information involve government information that has been removed from government websites (scrubbing), restrictions on the release and availability of "sensitive" government information, and increased difficulty for public libraries to identify and access certain types of government or other types of information requested by patrons.

Numerous information policy areas, many of which are altered by the USA PATRIOT Act, have a direct impact on public library provision of services and resources (Jaeger and Burnett 2005; Jaeger et al. 2004). For example, libraries may restrict access to the records they keep and to whom they provide services under the fear that federal agents will demand access to user logs and other personal information regarding the use of services from their particular library. Federal agents may engage in wiretaps of selected telecommunications going into or out of the library to obtain information on suspected terrorists. If a librarian discloses that the federal government has issued a National Security Letter requesting access to library files, that librarian may face legal consequences.

These and other information policy issues have a significant impact on the degree to which patrons may feel comfortable seeking information through electronic means. Even if the information being sought by the government is harmless and innocent, patrons may worry that what they are seeking may be misinterpreted, or they simply may want to preserve their privacy.

PRIVACY

Understanding information policy related to privacy is critical for the success of Internet-enabled services by public libraries. Privacy raises many concerns for protecting patrons and library staff, and these concerns have been complicated by many laws and policies that place expectations on libraries to provide access to certain types of information or to preserve certain records should the government wish to see them (Adams et al. 2005).

In one example, patrons come to Florida public libraries to complete forms and obtain assistance from several programs administered by the Department of Children and Families. Selected public libraries partner with the department to assist in these e-government programs. As the librarians assist patrons to complete these forms, a range of personal information may become known to the them. How can librarians shield themselves from this information? To what degree (if any) do librarians infringe on federal, state, or local privacy policies by assisting patrons in this manner? To what degree are librarians liable should such information be released to third parties? This one example is replicated countless times as patrons rely on assistance from librarians to get information about sensitive personal health issues, apply for jobs, seek benefits, fill out tax and other government forms, e-mail, chat, and countless other activities that can reveal many private details of someone's life.

FILTERING ACCESS

CIPA requires public libraries that receive many types of E-rate or LSTA funding to place filters on all computers to protect children from online content deemed potentially harmful. Under CIPA, public schools and public libraries receiving certain kinds of federal funds are required to use filtering programs to protect children under age seventeen from harmful visual depictions on the Internet and to provide public notices and public hearings to increase public awareness of Internet safety.

Many libraries have fought against the filtering requirements of CIPA because they perceive that the requirements violate the principle of librarianship to provide equal access to information. These philosophical concerns are also tied to significant concerns about the effectiveness and functionality of the filters themselves, along with objections to the requirements to filter access by adult patrons and staff as well as minors (Cabe 2002; Goldstein 2002; Horowitz 2000; Minow 1997; Peltz 2002). In 2007, approximately one-third of public libraries refused to apply for E-rate or LSTA funds specifically to avoid CIPA requirements, a substantial increase from the 15.3% of libraries that did not apply for E-rate as a result of CIPA in 2006 (Bertot, McClure, and Jaeger 2008). As a result of defending patrons' rights to free access, the libraries that are not applying for E-rate funds because of CIPA requirements are being forced to turn down the chance for funding to help pay for Internet access in order to preserve community access to the Internet. Because many libraries feel that they cannot apply for E-rate funds, different levels of Internet access are available to patrons of public libraries in different parts of the country (Jaeger, Bertot, et al. 2007).

PUBLIC ACCESS

Public policies can present challenges to libraries attempting to provide specific information and services through the Internet. Consider government information itself. The United States Code outlines a range of laws related to public access to and the role of the depository library program in the provision of government information (especially Title 44). Because many of the sections of the code have not been updated for the electronic, networked environment and the provision of e-government services, existing policies administered by the Government Printing Office (GPO) may complicate public library provision of e-government resources and services. Indeed, some GPO policies are so out-dated in the age of the Internet that one of the requirements for the head of the GPO is to be well skilled in the art of book binding.

There are provisions of the E-government Act, especially Chapter 36 (Man-agement and Promotion of Electronic Government Services), that appear to bypass a range of information policies and regulations regarding public access that traditionally have been under the jurisdiction of the GPO. And despite numerous federal and state agencies that either require or recommend use of public libraries in agency regulations, there is no mention of a role for public libraries in e-government in the E-government Act. How these ambiguities and possible contradictions are interpreted affects the success with which public libraries can provide e-government services.

INTELLECTUAL PROPERTY

The extension of copyright protection to such lengths—life of the author plus eighty years—creates many questions of ownership. Such conflicts are mag-nified by the increase in access to information brought about by the Internet and electronic files. The exceptions created to try to address these issues, such as the fair use exemption and the exemptions for use in distance education, only serve to make the issues murkier and leave many libraries confused (But-ler 2003; Travis 2006). Orphan works—older works for which the copyright owner is untraceable—are virtually unusable, even by archives that own the items (Brito and Dooling 2006; Carlson 2005).

Libraries have to work hard to avoid infringing on the intellectual prop-erty rights of many parties, including the vendors that provide digital content. Libraries struggle mightily with what previously were much clearer issues of interlibrary loan, electronic resources, and services to distance learners, and universities must determine how to provide resources to distance education students (Allner 2004; Carrico and Smalldon 2004; Ferullo 2004; Gasaway 2000). At the same time, libraries must also struggle with the implications of electronic files and the ability to share files for music, movies, books, and other content formats (Strickland 2003, 2004). Clearly, all of these issues complicate the provision of Internet access and services in public libraries.

OVERCOMING CHALLENGES

Ultimately, policy challenges not only affect the library's ability to use its technol-ogy to best fulfill social roles and expectations, they can challenge the position of the library itself. Only a small portion of public libraries used filters prior to CIPA (McCarthy 2004). Since the advent of computers in libraries, librarians have typi-cally used informal monitoring practices to ensure that nothing age inappropriate or morally offensive is publicly visible (Estabrook and Lakner 2000). Some state library systems, such as Kansas and Indiana, even developed formal or informal statewide approaches (Comer 2005; Reddick 2004).

The Supreme Court's holding regarding CIPA reflects several misconceptions about libraries, adopting an attitude that "we know what is best for you" (Gathegi 2005, 12). The Court assumes that libraries select printed materials out of a desire to protect and censor rather than recognizing the basic reality that only a small number of print materials can be afforded by any library. Though the Internet frees libraries from many of the costs associated with print materials, the Court assumes that libraries should censor the Internet as well, ultimately upholding the same level of access to information for adult patrons and librarians in public libraries as students in school libraries. Further, since filtering software companies make the decisions about how their products work, content and collection decisions for electronic resources in school and public libraries have been taken out of the hands of librarians and local communities and placed in the trust of proprietary software products (McCarthy 2004).

These types of misunderstandings of the capacities of and current social roles of libraries, reflected in public policy, are aggravated by the resistance in the public library community to acknowledging the importance of Internet-enabled roles and expectations for libraries. There are significant gaps between public policy and technology, which are only growing as the United States continues to make laws reactively and based on a pre-electronic mentality (Braman 2006). The gaps between policies and technological realities are becoming so significant that arguments can be made that information policies may have to be completely rethought (Travis 2006).

Public libraries are at the center of many of the debates regarding these policy issues. Yet, for all the difficulties associated with ensuring Internet access, training, and services, they have given public libraries the opportunity to take on increased importance to their communities in new ways. By the late 1990s, the social role for public libraries as a marketplace of ideas was already clearly being augmented by the public library's burgeoning social role as a safety net for accessing Internet services to limit gaps in access (McClure, Jaeger, and Bertot 2007). From its initial appearance, the Internet has suffered gaps in access related to social networks, geography, income level, ethnic type, educational attainment, and other factors, leading to a large number of residents being unable to access Internet services except through the public library (Burnett and Jaeger 2008; Burnett, Jaeger, and Thompson 2008; Jaeger and Thompson 2003, 2004). To ensure the social role as a marketplace of ideas, public libraries have embraced a new social role as a guarantor of public access to Internet service to all and then adopted new Internet-enabled service roles like e-government provider and emergency response and recovery center (see figure 5).

To confront challenges posed by public policy most effectively, all members of the public library community need to accept and acknowledge the vital importance of Internet-enabled service roles and expectations to the societal meaning of public libraries. A unified front in evaluating, assessing, studying, and describing the evolving social roles, Internet-enabled service roles, and expectations of public libraries will greatly help libraries positively impact the policy process and educate the public and policymakers of libraries' significant value to society.

Internet-enabled service roles are now a central component of public library services and societal expectations for the public library. Technology is now a driver of public library services, and one that is not going away. Recognition of Internet-enabled roles within all quarters of the library community and by public policy developers will greatly assist libraries to meet patron, community, and government expectations.

12

Roles and Expectations in Research, Education, and Advocacy

This book raises many issues related to the shift in social roles, service roles, expectations for, and the professional values of librarianship brought about by the provision of Internet access, training, and services. But the data and ideas in this book ultimately identify many more questions than they answer. In this chapter we offer a selection of key areas that could profit from additional research and discuss education and advocacy considerations for libraries and LIS programs. These considerations are intended to provide a larger context in which the issues raised in this book can be considered and approached by library professionals, students, scholars, policymakers, and educators.

AREAS OF RESEARCH

The findings and issues described in this book clearly demonstrate that there is still much work needed to describe and elucidate the use of social roles and Internet-enabled service roles in public libraries, including the following:

> *Clarification of concepts.* This book uses the phrase *public library social roles* to mean broad-based societal values and goals to which the library contributes. The phrase *service roles and responses* refers to more specific activities intended to assist public libraries in the planning process and to meet community expectations. *Internet-enabled service roles* are a type of public library service role that emphasizes digital or electronic access and services via the Internet. The degree to which these or perhaps other types of public library roles exist must be investigated.

Definition of social roles in public libraries. A cornerstone of this research is to better define the idea of *social roles in public libraries.* This book uses the following definition: The social roles of public libraries can be understood as the ways, intentionally or otherwise, public libraries affect the patrons and the surrounding communities. The literature, however, also uses such terms as *service roles, service responses,* and others. Some agreement on the meaning of *social roles* in public libraries is essential to continue research in related areas.

Identification of social roles in public libraries over the years. As one tracks the history of public libraries in the United States, can we identify each of the specific social roles the library has assumed? To what degree have public library social roles changed over the history of the country, and what factors appear to serve as catalysts for this change? Have these changes in social roles been directed from within the profession, or are they the result of external social, economic, or political factors?

Perceived importance of public library social and service roles. Do public librarians believe that it is important for the local library to have a clear understanding of the social and service roles it serves or is promoting (either formally or informally)? Does the presence of clear social and service roles in the local library promote the well-being and overall health of the library? An interesting study would compare funding success or other factors with the presence of planning documents that include clearly articulated service roles. In short, is the library better positioned to seek support when it has clear service roles that are understandable and promoted to the local community?

Regional differences in public library social and service roles. To what degree do public libraries in the Southeast, for example, have similar or different social and service roles than libraries in, for example, the Northwest? Such studies would explore how local or regional f actors are related to the social and service roles libraries might select for their community. They might also help explain the conditions under which some social roles are more or less important in a region or even a state.

Role of professional associations in promoting service roles. Since 1987, the PLA has formally promoted certain service roles for public libraries. What was the involvement of the ALA and PLA in developing and promoting such roles prior to 1987? To what degree have state library associations or other professional associations been involved in the development and promotion of these roles? Do these vary across different types of professional associations?

Public library social roles and public policy. Federal and state governments actively manage a range of information policy issues that either directly or indirectly affect public libraries. Has the federal government promoted (intentionally or unintentionally) certain social roles for public libraries, and with what effect? One can argue, for example, that the USA PATRIOT Act pushes public libraries into a social role of protecting society from terrorists, and that CIPA encourages public libraries to assist parents (or others) in ensuring that children are not placed in contact with pornography. Related to this topic is the degree to which public librarians have successfully promoted certain social roles with the government—such as the effort in the 1950s to have the Library Services and Construction Act funded?

Use of public library service roles since 1987. To what degree have public libraries used the various planning service roles first introduced in 1987 and revised in 2001 and 2007? An analysis of public library planning documents over this period might be especially instructive as to whether the service roles were used, which ones tended to be selected, and the degree to which the library demonstrated that the service roles were implemented and made a difference in the local community.

Use of Internet-enabled service roles. Although public libraries may not refer to the Internet-enabled service roles as named in this book (see figure 5), a study to determine the extent to which these service roles are in fact being delivered to the community would also be of interest. To what degree have Internet-enabled service roles replaced, augmented, or otherwise modified traditional public library service roles?

Impact and benefit measures of public library Internet-enabled services on users, families, and communities. Considerable attention has been given over the years to measuring benefits and impacts of traditional public library service roles, but Internet-enabled services have seen less analysis. Recent efforts to address the measurement and evaluation of Internet-enabled services did not consider the PLA service roles (Bertot and Davis 2004; Bertot, McClure, and Ryan 2001).

These topics only begin to suggest fertile ground for additional research in this area. Just a few of many other potential research issues include the following:

- demographics of users of traditional versus Internet-enabled service roles in public libraries
- relationships between user and community demographic factors and user and community impacts due to computer and Internet-enabled service roles
- impacts on libraries, users, families, and communities caused by inclusion or exclusion of Internet-enabled service roles

Given the recent history (since 1987) of formal attention to social and service roles by the PLA and others, a better understanding of these roles in public libraries and their impact on larger society may be critical to the success with which public libraries position themselves in the evolving Internet and networked environment.

EDUCATION ISSUES

As result of changes in roles and expectations for libraries, LIS programs must begin to adapt educational programs to better prepare students for the realities of the Internet-enabled public library. There are several key tasks that LIS schools need to face in order to ensure that future generations of librarians are educated to meet the Internet-related access, resource, and training roles and expectations of patrons, communities, and governments, including these:

Create master's level coursework that can more effectively prepare LIS students to provide Internet training, services, and tools in public libraries. LIS graduates joining the profession of public librarians must have a fundamental understanding of the centrality of the Internet to library services and patron expectations. Schools need to focus on training librarians who understand the professional, social, economic, usage, community, patron, and government issues associated with Internet access in public libraries. Educational approaches and strategies should be shared widely within the LIS profession to allow other schools and libraries themselves to begin training librarians in these areas.

Increase the number of LIS faculty and library professionals ready to meet these roles and expectations. LIS students schooled in these roles and expectations will spread what they learn by sharing this knowledge in professional contexts. Some MLS students will become PhD students as well. LIS doctoral students who are educated about these roles and expectations will become faculty members who continue to teach and research these areas at other LIS programs. This, in turn, will dramatically increase the number of schools where MLS students—as future practitioners and administrators—will be educated in issues related to the intersection of public libraries and the Internet. Ultimately, this will enable a much greater number of public libraries to meet social and service roles and expectations related to the Internet.

Develop means to share ideas and best practices between libraries. As a result of insufficient research and teaching in this area, public libraries are not able to effectively coordinate approaches, share ideas, or identify best practices. More LIS schools teaching their students about these roles and expectations will ultimately facilitate the development of larger initiatives in services, resources, and training that can span the initiatives of individual public libraries.

Conduct research that advances understanding about and creates practical solutions for public libraries in meeting Internet-enabled service roles and expectations. More practical LIS research is needed to help libraries in their Internet-related roles. Research topics include the impacts of Internet roles and services on library patrons; the most effective ways to meet the needs of diverse patron populations; the development of tools for libraries to use in these new roles and services; ways to determine and fulfill community expectations for Internet-related access, training, and services; and managerial strategies in the meeting of these new roles and expectations.

Increase the number of LIS faculty members who specialize in the intersections of public libraries and the Internet. Preparing future LIS faculty members with deep knowledge and understanding of the roles and impacts of the Internet on public library management, services, patrons, community and government expectations, and other issues will be a significant step in the education of future librarians. This knowledge can be passed on to master's level students who are planning to work in public libraries, thus better preparing them to meet the information needs of twenty-first-century patrons.

There are different educational programs or specializations that could arise from these broad areas. For example, the College of Information Studies at the University of Maryland has launched its E-government Master's Concentration (http://ischool.umd.edu/programs/egov.shtml). This program is unique among LIS schools and, in fact, is one of the few graduate programs devoted to e-government in any field internationally. Students can enroll to study the nature and use of e-government information; policies and laws shaping e-government; management, economic, and social challenges to providing e-government access; and other issues related to e-government. The core issues and intersections of librarianship and e-government are diffused throughout the courses in the program curriculum.

To complement the E-government Master's Concentration, the college has also established the Center for Information Policy and Electronic Government (CIPEG), a multidisciplinary research and educational facility devoted to the study of e-government and its implications for governments and citizens (www.cipeg.umd.edu). Through CIPEG, students in the E-government Master's Concentration are able to interact with researchers and practitioners in e-government and work on actual research projects related to e-government, such as user studies and library surveys.

These efforts at the University of Maryland represent but one of seemingly limitless opportunities for LIS programs to develop courses, programs of study, research centers, and degrees that will help prepare students for the roles and expectations they will encounter as professionals. Some other LIS programs are beginning to explore these options. For example, master's students at the School of Information at the University of Michigan can take a course in digital government as part of the Information Policy Specialization in the MS in Information program (http://si.umich.edu/msi/ipol.htm). All of these educational efforts can be significant in creating more research to document and analyze the impacts these roles and expectations have on libraries, librarians, patrons, communities, and governments.

Advocacy Based on Internet Roles and Expectations

Along with pursuing educational programs that help librarians meet new roles and expectations, public libraries must also become more involved in the policy-making process and in seeking financial and other support for these activities. Public libraries have to demand a voice not only to better convey their critical role in the provision of Internet access, training, and services but to help shape the direction of policymaking to ensure more government support for these activities, including specific functions like e-government and emergency response.

Public libraries have taken on the Internet-enabled responsibilities detailed in this book without receiving additional funding for their efforts. For example, while the provision of Internet access is itself a major expense for public libraries, the reliance of government agencies on public libraries as the public support system for e-government adds significant extra burdens to libraries (Bertot, McClure, and Jaeger 2008; Jaeger and Fleischmann 2007). In a 2007 survey of Florida public libraries, 98.7% indicated that they received no support from an outside agency to support the e-government services the library provides, despite the fact that 83.3% of responding libraries indicated that the use of e-government in the library had increased overall library usage (McClure et al. 2007). This lack of outside support has resulted in public libraries in different parts of the country having widely varying access to e-government services (Jaeger, forthcoming; Jaeger, Bertot, et al. 2007).

The reality is that public libraries are expected by patrons, communities, and government agencies to fulfill a wide range of Internet-enabled service roles, whether or not any support—financial, staffing, or training—is provided to meet these expectations. Public libraries need to become more actively involved in and encourage plans and programs that serve to sustain these major social roles while also bringing some level of financial, training, and staffing support for these roles.

The hurricane seasons of 2004 and 2005 resoundingly demonstrated how much the Internet has changed community expectations of libraries and library capacities to actually help their communities. The extensive efforts and successes of public libraries in the aftermath of the hurricanes has earned libraries a central position in e-government and emergency planning at local, state, and federal levels. In those emergency situations, public libraries were able to serve their communities in a capacity far beyond the traditional image of the role of libraries, but these emergency response roles are as significant as anything else libraries could do for their communities. The success of libraries in these and other emergency situations has created expectations that they will be able to perform similarly in future emergencies in spite of their lack of integration into the traditional emergency response structures and systems (Jaeger, Fleischmann et al. 2007; Jaeger, Shneiderman et al. 2007). To continue to fulfill these roles and adequately perform other expected functions, public libraries need to push not only for financial support but also for a greater role in planning and decision making related to Internet access and e-government services as well as to emergency response and recovery at all levels of government.

If strategic plans and library activities have a consistent message about the need for support, the related roles of the marketplace of ideas and the guarantor of Internet access can make a compelling argument for increases in funding, support, and social standing of public libraries. The most obvious source of further support for these activities would be the federal government. Amazingly, federal government support accounts for only about 1% of total public library funding (Bertot, Jaeger, et al. 2006b). Given that federal government agencies are already relying on public libraries to ensure access to e-government and foster community response and recovery in times of emergencies, among many other Internet-enabled roles and services, federal support for these social roles and services of the public library clearly can and should be increased significantly.

State libraries, cooperatives, and library networks already work to coordinate funding and activities related to certain programs, like the E-rate program. These same library collectives may be able to work together to promote the need for additional resources and coordinate those resources once they are attained. Private and public partnerships offer another means of support for these library activities. With its strong historical and current connections to technology and libraries, the Bill and Melinda Gates Foundation might be an important partner in funding and facilitating the increased roles public libraries are taking on in the age of the Internet. The search for additional funding to support these roles and services should focus on funds not only for access and training but also for research about how to better meet individual and community needs and the impacts of Internet provision by public libraries on individuals and communities.

Regardless of what approaches are taken to find greater support, however, public libraries must do a better job of communicating their Internet-enabled roles and services to governments and private organizations in order to increase support from them. Such communications must be part of a larger strategy to define a place within public policy that gives public libraries a voice in related policy issues. If public libraries are going to fulfill these social roles, they must become a greater presence in the national policy discourse surrounding issues such as telecommunications policy, e-government, and emergency response. To increase their support and their standing in policy discourse, libraries must not be hesitant in reminding the public and government officials of their successes in ensuring universal access to the Internet, supporting emergency response and recovery, providing the social infrastructure for e-filing of taxes and enrolling in Medicare prescription drug plans, and myriad other routine Internet-enabled activities.

It seems unlikely, however, that the same government officials pushing the use of e-government in public libraries are aware of the roles of public libraries in helping citizens with day-to-day use of e-government. Further, the enormous social roles of public libraries in emergency response in communities, such as during the 2004 and 2005 hurricane seasons, are not widely known among government officials. To encourage the provision of external funding and policy support for these social roles, public libraries must make the government and the public better aware of these roles and what is needed to ensure that the roles are fulfilled.

13

Roles and Expectations and the Future of Public Libraries

As the Internet brings sizable changes to the central roles and expectations for public libraries in society, it is important to keep in mind how much the public library has changed as a social institution in little more than a century and, more astounding, within the past twenty years. The Internet has produced a major expansion of the social and service roles public libraries play in the lives of patrons, in the activities of communities, and in service to governments. These changes have taken place so quickly that it can be hard to appreciate how much has happened and how large the impacts are on the public library.

It is easy to imagine that things were simpler or purer when libraries were a repository of books alone. Consider, though, the early professional debates regarding the social roles of libraries described in chapter 2—in which the first primary set of social roles embraced by public librarians was unwaveringly prescriptive. At the first ALA meeting in 1876, "most agreed that the mass reading public was generally incapable of choosing its own reading materials judiciously" (Wiegand 1976, 10). Civic and political leaders believed that public libraries could provide a civilizing influence on the masses and be a means to shape the populace into adhering to hegemonic standards (Augst 2001; Garrison 1993; Harris 1973, 1976). This attitude was reflected in the elitist and paternalistic attitudes of most public libraries in selecting materials for the public betterment and in attempting to be social stewards of the general population (Augst 2001; Heckart 1991; Wiegand 1996).

Although these attitudes have obviously evolved rather dramatically in subsequent years, there is always the risk of resistance, overreaction, or confusion when a new major change occurs. The rise of Internet-enabled roles and expectations as an essential part of the public library in the minds of patrons, communities, and governments is, without question, a major change. But it has also become established as a central part of public libraries that is not going away anytime soon. A public library without electronic resources is now akin to a public library without print materials; neither is going to meet the expectations of patrons or fulfill the social roles expected of the library.

When public libraries first began to embrace the Internet, there was hope that the Internet could serve as a means of supporting and augmenting their established social roles as marketplaces of ideas. In 1998 it was suggested that "the advent of commodified information makes the communication of a public library service essential for the protection of citizenship, which is the basis of many democratic political systems" (Kerslake and Kinnell 1998, 166). And, as predicted, not only does the library have new roles—such as a means of daily communication through e-mail and a key part of community emergency response in extreme circumstances—the traditional roles have expanded greatly because of the capacities of the Internet.

Many libraries are emphasizing Internet-enabled service roles as a part of established or new social roles that have redefined the purpose of the public library. The role of provider of access to educational materials now includes electronic databases and the ability for patrons to take online courses at the library. The role of support for job seeking now includes assisting patrons to search for and apply for jobs online and use library computers to set up e-mail accounts to communicate with potential employers. The role of provider of government information now includes the wealth of e-government information and services that can be accessed and completed in the library. These are just a few examples; many others are detailed throughout this book. As we suggest throughout, however, those connections are generally not being met as well as they could be and are even being resisted in some quarters.

On the other extreme, some may wish to expand the argument in this book by suggesting that the established public library social roles are antiquated and inappropriate for public libraries in a networked environment. The vast changes in access to and use of Internet-related technologies may be marginalizing public libraries' traditional social roles and, thus, their perceived importance in the local community. The varying degrees to which libraries integrate Internet-enabled public library service roles into clear social roles appropriate for the networked environment may help to explain libraries' varying success at gaining local support—depending on the situational factors at a particular public library.

Given the range of perspectives on these issues, the public library community needs to engage in a substantive national discussion about the appropriate social roles for public libraries in the networked environment and the service implications of these social roles—such as those outlined by the PLA in 2007 and those offered in figure 5. It is clear that patrons, communities, and governments have major expectations for the Internet-enabled roles of public libraries, and it behooves all members of the public library community to work together to reconcile different approaches to and perceptions of the roles public libraries are now expected to fulfill.

Currently, there may be a disconnect among the broad social roles of public libraries, such as the library as a marketplace of ideas; the traditional service roles and responses offered in 1987, 2001, and 2007 by the PLA; and the Internet-enabled service roles and responses described earlier in this book. Public libraries face a conundrum of competing demands and responsibilities for how best to respond to changing society and community expectations of the public library in the networked environment. As public librarians plan for the provision of services, this conundrum may result in a path of least resistance that provides more public-access workstations, wireless access, and greater bandwidth—without careful thought as to how such access will be used as service roles and responses.

The Internet provides numerous opportunities to support established social roles and create new ones. If effectively coordinated with established roles, it clearly can support and enhance the value of the public library to the community. The traditional roles, as they have evolved, are obviously complemented and enhanced by the Internet. However, by failing to integrate adequately the Internet-enabled roles into the established roles or by emphasizing the provision of Internet-enabled roles at the expense of traditional roles, public libraries may be significantly altering the broader roles they play in society in unintended ways or even undermining their own efforts to fulfill the expectations of patrons, communities, and governments.

The ways in which Internet-enabled roles affect the broader social roles public libraries are trying to fulfill need to be the focus of greater debate, discussion, and investigation to ensure that new public library social roles related to Internet services complement and promote established social roles and extend the importance and impact of public libraries in society. The extent to which public libraries can continue to maintain traditional service roles and expand Internet-enabled service roles is a question of vital importance to the profession. Clarifying the larger social roles public libraries should serve in the Internet-based society is an important discussion that may have long-term impacts on the health and sustainability of public libraries in the future—a future that in the near term will continue to be Internet driven.

Librarians can undertake specific strategies to better understand and respond to the move toward Internet-enabled service roles and responses. First, as previously described, key research that better describes the current situation regarding public library societal and service roles is needed. Based on findings from such research efforts, it is likely several initiatives could be developed:

- Plan for and conduct regional/state meetings or open hearings around the country to discuss issues related to public library social roles and obtain practical information about how Internet-enabled roles and responses are being developed and implemented. Leadership in this effort by the PLA, state libraries, and others could bring significant attention to these meetings.

- Use the development of Internet-enabled service roles and responses in public libraries to better argue for the importance of public libraries at the local level—describing and measuring the various benefits and impacts provided to the local community as a result of these service roles. This would be an important accomplishment.

- Work with local, state, and federal government officials to determine how Internet-enabled service roles and responses can best be financed and how these roles can be developed cooperatively to support digital democracy and e-government services. A key aspect of these efforts will be better articulating and demonstrating to politicians and policymakers the major impacts of the Internet-enabled roles of public libraries in everyday and extreme circumstances.

- Confront and make sense of the federal, local, and state policies enveloping the Internet-enabled public library. Specific policy and legislation related to the financing efforts mentioned above must be explored. The larger policy context that creates so many challenges must be analyzed and should be untangled to ensure that public policy does not inhibit public libraries from meeting the roles and expectations of society.

- Develop web-based instructional and communications materials and forums to continue to explore aspects of Internet-enabled public library service roles. These online tools could include descriptions of Internet-enabled service roles being used in public libraries, methods for assessing these roles, blogs and wikis to exchange views about the service roles, updates of roles currently being used or developed, and other information.

- Revise and update the formalized public library Internet-enabled service roles and responses to better recognize those activities in which public libraries are already engaged and to assist libraries to move into locally designed Internet-enabled service roles more quickly and effectively.

- Promote educational initiatives, programs, and degrees related to Internet-enabled public library roles in LIS programs. New library professionals must be prepared to work and thrive in an environment of Internet-enabled roles and expectations.

- Educate and inform community members. Libraries need to work to emphasize how significant the Internet-enabled roles can be in everyday needs (finding tax forms), in assisting in life events (finding a new job), and in community-wide emergencies. Support from individual community members will encourage more tangible forms of support from governments and perhaps even greater respect.

These are but a few specific strategies that can be considered in promoting the importance of Internet-enabled service roles and responses provided by public libraries for their local communities.

The data and evidence referred to in this book are not static, and neither are the Internet-related initiatives of public libraries. The service and social roles of public libraries in the age of the Internet will continue to evolve as technology and expectations about technology change. How they evolve will be seen in future research and study of public libraries. These changes should continue to be monitored.

As this book was being completed, several new data sets reinforced the themes of the book. A study released in December 2007 found that Internet users were more likely than nonusers to seek information from the public library (Estabrook, Witt, and Rainie 2007). A study released in February 2008 showed that public libraries evoke high levels of trust and that the public sees significant benefits in the Internet-enabled services they provide (Griffiths and King 2008). Both studies demonstrate the importance of the library as a trusted source of Internet-enabled resources by diverse user groups of many ages.

Perhaps most telling, however, are new data from the ALA's *Public Library Funding and Technology Access Study* (American Library Association and Information Institute 2008). Between 2007 and 2008, there have been significant increases in the provision of many Internet-enabled resources by public libraries. The new survey data indicate double-digit growth from 2007 to 2008 in the provision of resources in five key online service areas:

- Audio content increased from 38% to 71%.
- Video content from 16.6% to 48.9%.
- Homework resources from 68.1% to 83.4%.
- E-book availability from 38.3% to 51.8%.
- Digitized special collections from 21.1% to 33.8%.

These findings reinforce not only the centrality of the Internet to public library roles but the strong link between societal Internet-enabled service expectations and the public library.

Additional data will continue to be generated by independent researchers and through institutional sources such as the ALA, IMLS, Bill and Melinda Gates Foundation, Pew Internet and the American Life Project, U.S. Census Bureau, and others. Internet-based public library service roles and the changes in society they document will need to be reconsidered continually and analyzed in light of such new data.

Ultimately, at issue is the long-term health and success of public libraries as they continue to evolve in an electronic, networked, and Internet-based society. Finding balance between traditional and Internet-enabled service roles and responses that recognizes local situational factors will be a key challenge for public libraries in the future. But recognizing that public libraries are in fact currently providing and can extend a vast array of Internet-enabled service roles and responses is equally important. The partnership between public libraries and the Internet can be expanded and promoted for the benefit of both public libraries and society at large. It can also help to convey to the public, to funding agencies, and to policymakers the true value of public libraries to society.

Change can be unsettling, but it can also be exhilarating and lead to better libraries and library services. The Internet-enabled public library has much greater social capacities and capabilities than the library of exclusively print materials. Librarians of fifty years ago could not have imagined that the public library could instantly provide access to government information at the press of a button or play a vital role in helping a devastated region recover from a great natural disaster, but they undoubtedly would have been enthusiastic about these opportunities to serve society in these critical ways. The task at hand, then, is to ensure that the public library remains a vibrant marketplace of ideas freely accessible to all members of the community while recognizing the importance of the Internet and seamlessly incorporating Internet-enabled roles and expectations that have greatly expanded what a public library can provide to society.

References

Adams, H. R., R. F. Bocher, C. A. Gordon, and E. Barry-Kessler. 2005. *Privacy in the 21st century: Issues for public, school, and academic libraries.* Westport, CT: Libraries Unlimited.

Allner, I. 2004. Copyright and the delivery of library services to distance learners. *Internet Reference Services Quarterly* 9 (3): 179–192.

American Library Association. 2002. U.S. Supreme Court arguments on CIPA expected in late winter or early spring. www.ala.org/ala/pressreleasesbucket/ussupremecourt.cfm.

American Library Association and Information Institute. 2007. *Libraries connect communities: Public library funding and technology access study 2006–2007.* Chicago: American Library Association.

———. 2008. *Libraries connect communities: Public library funding and technology access study 2007–2008.* Chicago: American Library Association.

Augst, T. 2001. Introduction: Libraries and agencies of culture. In *Libraries as agencies of culture,* ed. T. Augst and W. Wiegand. Madison: University of Wisconsin Press.

Baker, N. 1996. The author vs. the library. *New Yorker* 72 (31): 51–62.

———. 2001. *Double fold: Libraries and the assault on paper.* New York: Random House.

Bardket, P. 2007. *How to use Web 2.0 in your library.* New York: Neal Shuman.

Bennett, S. 2001. The golden age of libraries. *Journal of Academic Librarianship* 27 (4): 256–259.

Berninghausen, D. K. 1953. The history of the ALA intellectual freedom committee. *Wilson Library Bulletin* 27 (10): 813–817.

Bertot, J. C., and D. M. Davis. 2004. *Planning and evaluating library networked services and resources.* Westport, CT: Libraries Unlimited.

Bertot, J. C., P. T. Jaeger, L. A. Langa, and C. R. McClure. 2006a. Public access computing and Internet access in public libraries: The role of public libraries in e-government and emergency situations. *First Monday* 11 (9). www.firstmonday.org/issues/issue11_9/bertot/index.html.

———. 2006b. Drafted: I want you to deliver e-government. *Library Journal* 131 (13): 34–39.

Bertot, J. C., and C. R. McClure. 2007. Assessing the sufficiency and quality of bandwidth for public libraries. *Information Technology and Libraries* 26 (1): 14–22.

Bertot, J. C., C. R. McClure, and P. T. Jaeger. 2005. Public libraries struggle to meet Internet demand: New study shows libraries need support to sustain technology services. *American Libraries* 36 (7): 78–79.

———. 2008. The impacts of free public Internet access on public library patrons and communities. *Library Quarterly* 78 (3): 285–301.

Bertot, J. C., C. R. McClure, P. T. Jaeger, and J. Ryan. 2006. *Public libraries and the Internet 2006: Study results and findings.* Tallahassee, FL: Information Institute.

Bertot, J. C., C. R. McClure, and J. Ryan. 2001. *Statistics and performance measures for public library networked services.* Chicago: American Library Association.

Bertot, J. C., C. R. McClure, S. Thomas, K. M. Barton, and J. McGilvray. 2007. *Public libraries and the Internet 2007: Report to the American Library Association.* Tallahassee, FL: Information Institute.

Bourke, C. 2005. Public libraries building social capital through networking. *Australasian Public Libraries and Information Services* 18 (2): 71–75.

Braman, S. 2006. *Change of state: Information, policy, and power.* Cambridge, MA: MIT Press.

Brito, J., and B. Dooling. 2006. Who's your daddy? *Wall Street Journal,* March 25, A9.

Brophy, P. 2007. *The library in the twenty-first century.* 2nd ed. London: Facet.

Brown, J. S., and P. Duguid. 2002. *The social life of information.* Boston: Harvard Business School Press.

Burke, S. K., and E. Martin. 2004. Libraries in communities: Expected and unexpected portrayals in state case law. *Libraries and Culture* 39:405–428.

Burnett, G., and P. T. Jaeger. 2008. Small worlds, lifeworlds, and information: The ramifications of the information behaviors of social groups in public policy and the public sphere. *Information Research* 13 (2). http://InformationR.net/ir/13-2/paper346.html.

Burnett, G., P. T. Jaeger, and K. M. Thompson. 2008. The social aspects of information access: The viewpoint of normative theory of information behavior. *Library and Information Science Research* 30:56–66.

Buschman, J. E. 2003. *Dismantling the public sphere: Situating and sustaining librarianship in the age of the new public philosophy.* Westport, CT: Libraries Unlimited.

Buschman, J. E., and G. J. Leckie, eds. 2007. *The library as place: History, community, and culture.* Westport, CT: Libraries Unlimited.

Butler, R. P. 2003. Copyright law and organizing the Internet. *Library Trends* 52 (2): 307–317.

Cabe, T. 2002. Regulation of speech on the Internet: Fourth time's the charm? *Media Law and Policy* 11:50–61.

Carlson, S. 2005. Whose work is it, anyway? *Chronicle of Higher Education* 51 (47): A33–A35.

Carr, D. W. 2003. An ethos of trust in information service. In *Ethics and electronic information: A festschrift for Stephen Almagno,* ed. B. Rockenbach, and T. Mendina, 45–52. Jefferson, NC: McFarland.

Carrico, J. C., and K. L. Smalldon. 2004. Licensed to ILL: A beginning guide to negotiating e-resources licenses to permit resource sharing. *Journal of Library Administration* 40 (1/2): 41–54.

Casey, M. E., and L. C. Savastinuk. 2007. *Library 2.0: A guide to participatory library service.* Medford CT: Information Today.

Center for Creative Voices in Media. 2007. *The case for universal broadband in America: Now!* Keswick, VA: Center for Creative Voices in Media.

Cohen, J. M., A. L. Kelsey, and K. M. Fiels. 2001. *Planning for integrated systems and technologies.* New York: Neal Shuman.

Comer, A. D. 2005. Studying Indiana public libraries' usage of Internet filters. *Computers in Libraries,* June, 10–15.

Courtney, N., ed. 2005. *Technology for the rest of us: A primer on computer technologies for the low-tech librarian.* Westport, CT: Libraries Unlimited.

———. 2007. *Library 2.0 and beyond: Innovative technology and tomorrow's user.* Greenwood, CT: Libraries Unlimited.

Debono, B. 2002. Assessing the social impact of public libraries: What the literature is saying. *Australasian Public Libraries and Information Services* 15 (2): 80–95.

Dowell, D. R. 2008. The "i" in libraries. *American Libraries* 39 (1/2): 42.

Dresang, E. T. 2006. Intellectual freedom and libraries: Complexity and change in the twenty-first century digital environment. *Library Quarterly* 76:169–192.

Druin, A. 2005. What children can teach us: Developing digital libraries for children. *Library Quarterly* 75:20–41.

Economist. 1998. Off to the library: Buildings, books, and bytes. *Economist,* September 12, 30.

Estabrook, L., and E. Lakner. 2000. Managing Internet access: Results of a national survey. *American Libraries* 31:60–62.

Estabrook, L., E. Witt, and L. Rainie. 2007. *Information searches that solve problems: How people use the Internet, libraries, and government agencies when they need help.* New York: Pew Internet and American Life Project. December 20.

Ferullo, D. L. 2004. Major copyright issues in academic libraries: Legal implications of a digital environment. *Journal of Library Administration* 40 (1/2): 23–40.

Fiske, M. 1959. *Book selection and censorship: A study of school and public libraries in California.* Berkeley: University of California Press.

Fleischmann, K. R. 2007. Digital libraries with embedded values: Combining insights from LIS and science and technology studies. *Library Quarterly* 77:409–427.

Foerstel, H. N. 1991. *Surveillance in the stacks: The FBI's library awareness program.* Westport, CT: Greenwood.

———. 2004. *Refuge of a scoundrel: The PATRIOT Act in libraries.* Westport, CT: Greenwood.

Fourie, D. K., and D. R. Dowell. 2002. *Libraries in the information age: An introduction and career exploration.* Westport, CT: Libraries Unlimited.

Garcia, J., and S. Nelson. 2007. *2007 Public library service responses.* Chicago: Public Library Association.

Garrison, D. 1993. *Apostles of culture: The public librarian and American society, 1876–1920.* Madison: University of Wisconsin Press.

Gasaway, L. N. 2000. Values conflict in the digital environment: Librarians versus copyright holders. *Columbia—VLA Journal of Law and the Arts,* Fall, 115–161.

Gathegi, J. N. 2005. The public library and the (de)evolution of a legal doctrine. *Library Quarterly* 75:1–19.

Gellar, E. 1974. Intellectual freedom: Eternal principle or unanticipated consequence? *Library Journal* 99:1364–1367.

———. 1984. *Forbidden books in American public libraries, 1876–1939: A study in cultural change.* Westport, CT: Greenwood.

Given, L., and G. L. Leckie. 2003. "Sweeping" the library: Mapping the social activity space of the public library. *Library and Information Science Research* 25:365–385.

Goldstein, A. 2002. Like a sieve: The Children's Internet Protection Act and ineffective filters in libraries. *Fordham Intellectual Property, Media and Entertainment Journal* 12:1187–1202.

Gorman, M. 1997. *Our singular strengths: Meditations for librarians.* Chicago: American Library Association.

———. 2000. *Our enduring values: Librarianship in the 21st century.* Chicago: American Library Association.

———. 2005. *Our own selves: More meditations for librarians.* Chicago: American Library Association.

Goulding, A. 2004. Libraries and social capital. *Journal of Librarianship and Information Science* 36 (1): 3–6.

Gray, C. M. 1993. The civic role of libraries. In *Critical approaches to information technology in librarianship: Foundations and applications,* ed. J. E. Buschman. Westport, CT: Greenwood.

Griffiths, J.-M., and King, D. W. 2008. *Interconnections: The IMLS national study on the use of libraries, museums and the Internet.* Washington DC: Institute of Museum and Library Services.

Groen, F. K. 2007. *Access to medical knowledge: Libraries, digitization, and the public good.* Lanham, MD: Scarecrow.

Hafner, A. W. 1987. Public libraries and society in the information age. *Reference Librarian* 18:107–118.

Harris, M. H. 1973. The purpose of the American public library: A revisionist interpretation of history. *Library Journal* 98:2509–2514.

———. 1976. Public libraries and the decline of the democratic dogma. *Library Journal* 101:2225–2230.

Heckart, R. J. 1991. The library as marketplace of ideas. *College and Research Libraries* 52:491–505.

Hillenbrand, C. 2005. Public libraries as developers of social capital. *Australasian Public Libraries and Information Services* 18 (1): 4–12.

Himmel, E. E., and W. J. Willson. 1999. *Planning for results.* Chicago: American Library Association.

Horowitz, A. 2000. The constitutionality of the Children's Internet Protection Act. *St. Thomas Law Review* 13:425–444.

Horrigan, J. B. 2007. *A typology of information and communication users.* New York: Pew Foundation, Pew Internet and American Life Project.

Jaeger, P. T. Forthcoming. Public libraries and local e-government: Connection and education. In *Strategies for local e-government adoption and implementation: Comparative studies,* ed. C. G. Reddick. New York: IGI Global.

Jaeger, P. T., J. C. Bertot, and C. R. McClure. 2003. The impact of the USA Patriot Act on collection and analysis of personal information under the Foreign Intelligence Surveillance Act. *Government Information Quarterly* 20 (3): 295–314.

———. 2004. The effects of the Children's Internet Protection Act (CIPA) in public libraries and its implications for research: A statistical, policy, and legal analysis. *Journal of the American Society for Information Science and Technology* 55 (13): 1131–1139.

———. 2007. Public libraries and the Internet 2006: Issues, funding, and challenges. *Public Libraries* 46 (5): 71–78.

Jaeger, P. T., J. C. Bertot, C. R. McClure, and L. A. Langa. 2006. The policy implications of Internet connectivity in public libraries. *Government Information Quarterly* 23 (1): 123–141.

Jaeger, P. T., J. C. Bertot, C. R. McClure, and M. Rodriguez. 2007. Public libraries and Internet access across the United States: A comparison by state from 2004 to 2006. *Information Technology and Libraries* 26 (2): 4–14.

Jaeger, P. T., and G. Burnett. 2005. Information access and exchange among small worlds in a democratic society: The role of policy in redefining information behavior in the post-9/11 United States. *Library Quarterly* 75 (4): 464–495.

Jaeger, P. T., and K. R. Fleischmann. 2007. Public libraries, values, trust, and e-government. *Information Technology and Libraries* 26 (4): 35–43.

Jaeger, P. T., K. R. Fleischmann, J. Preece, B. Shneiderman, F. P. Wu, and Y. Qu. 2007. Community response grids: Facilitating community response to biosecurity and bioterror emergencies through information and communication technologies. *Biosecurity and Bioterrorism* 5 (4): 335–346.

Jaeger, P. T., L. A. Langa, C. R. McClure, and J. C. Bertot. 2006. The 2004 and 2005 Gulf Coast hurricanes: Evolving roles and lessons learned for public libraries in disaster preparedness and community services. *Public Library Quarterly* 25 (3/4): 199–214.

Jaeger, P. T., and C. R. McClure. 2004. Potential legal challenges to the application of the Children's Internet Protection Act (CIPA) in public libraries: Strategies and issues. *First Monday* 9 (2). www.firstmonday.org/issues/issue9_2/jaeger/index.html.

Jaeger, P. T., C. R. McClure, and J. C. Bertot. 2005. The E-rate program and libraries and library consortia, 2000–2004: Trends and issues. *Information Technology and Libraries* 24 (2): 57–67.

Jaeger, P. T., C. R. McClure, J. C. Bertot, and L. A. Langa. 2005. CIPA: Decisions, implementation, and impacts. *Public Libraries* 44 (2): 105–109.

Jaeger, P. T., C. R. McClure, J. C. Bertot, and J. T. Snead. 2004. The USA PATRIOT Act, the Foreign Intelligence Surveillance Act, and information policy research in libraries: Issues, impacts, and questions for library researchers. *Library Quarterly* 74 (2): 99–121.

Jaeger, P. T., B. Shneiderman, K. R. Fleischmann, J. Preece, Y. Qu, and F. P. Wu. 2007. Community response grids: E-government, social networks, and effective emergency response. *Telecommunications Policy* 31:592–604.

Jaeger, P. T., and K. M. Thompson. 2003. E-government around the world: Lessons, challenges, and new directions. *Government Information Quarterly* 20 (4): 389–394.

———. 2004. Social information behavior and the democratic process: Information poverty, normative behavior, and electronic government in the United States. *Library and Information Science Research* 26 (1): 94–107.

Jones, P. A., Jr. 1993. From censorship to intellectual freedom to empowerment: The evolution of the social responsibility of the American public library. *North Carolina Libraries* 52:135–137.

Kelton, K., K. R. Fleischmann, and W. A. Wallace. 2008. Trust in digital information. *Journal of the American Society for Information Science and Technology* 59 (3): 363–374.

Kerslake, E., and M. Kinnell. 1998. Public libraries, public interest and the information society: Theoretical issues in the social impact of public libraries. *Journal of Librarianship and Information Science* 30 (3): 159–167.

Kranich, N. 2001. Libraries, the Internet, and democracy. In *Libraries and democracy: The cornerstones of liberty,* ed. N. Kranich, 83–95. Chicago: American Library Association.

Lancaster, F. W., ed. 1993. *Libraries and the future: Essays on the library in the twenty-first century.* New York: Haworth.

Lankes, R. D., J. Silverstein, and S. Nicholson. 2007. Participatory networks: The library as conversation. *Information Technology and Libraries* 26 (4): 17–33.

Leckie, G. J., and J. Hopkins. 2002. The public place of central libraries: Findings from Toronto and Vancouver. *Library Quarterly* 72:326–372.

Manoff, M. 2001. The symbolic meaning of libraries in a digital age. *portal: Libraries and the Academy* 1:371–381.

Matthews, J. R. 2004a. *Measuring for results: The dimensions of public library effectiveness.* Westport, CT: Libraries Unlimited.

———. 2004b. *Technology planning: Preparing and updating a library technology plan.* Westport, CT: Libraries Unlimited.

———. 2007. *The evaluation and measurement of library services.* Westport, CT: Libraries Unlimited.

Mayo, D. 2005. *Technology for results: Developing service-based plans.* Chicago: American Library Association.

Mayo, D., and S. Nelson. 1999. *Wired for the future: Developing your library technology plan.* Chicago: American Library Association.

McCarthy, M. M. 2004. Filtering the Internet: The Children's Internet Protection Act. *Educational Horizons,* Winter, 108–113.

McChesney, K. 1984. History of libraries, librarianship, and library education. In *The library in society,* ed. A. R. Rogers and K. McChesney, 33–60. Littleton, CO: Libraries Unlimited.

McClure, C. R. 1993. Updating planning and role setting for public libraries. *Public Libraries* 32 (July/August): 198–199.

———. 1996. Public libraries, the public interest, and the National Information Infrastructure (NII): Expanding the policy agenda. In *20/20 vision: The development of a National Information Infrastructure,* 137–153. Washington, DC: Department of Commerce, National Telecommunications and Information Administration.

———. 2008. Learning and using evaluation: A practical introduction. In *The portable MLIS: Insights from the experts,* ed. B. Sheldon. Westport CT: Libraries Unlimited.

McClure, C. R., J. C. Bertot, and D. L. Zweizig. 1994. *Public libraries and the Internet: Study results, policy issues, and recommendations.* Washington, DC: National Commission on Libraries and Information Science.

McClure, C. R., and P. T. Jaeger. Forthcoming. Government information policy research: Importance, approaches, and realities. *Library and Information Science Research.*

McClure, C. R., P. T. Jaeger, and J. C. Bertot. 2007. The looming infrastructure plateau? Space, funding, connection speed, and the ability of public libraries to meet the demand for free Internet access. *First Monday* 12 (12). www.uic.edu/htbin/cgiwrap/bin/ojs/index.php/fm/article/view/2017/1907.

McClure, C. R., J. McGilvray, K. M. Barton, and J. C. Bertot. 2007. *E-government and public libraries: Current status, meeting report, findings, and next steps.* Tallahassee, FL: Information Use Management and Policy Institute. www.ii.fsu.edu/announcements/e-gov2006/egov_report.pdf.

McClure, C. R., A. Owen, D. L. Zweizig, M. J. Lynch, and N. A. Van House. 1987. *Planning and role setting for public libraries: A manual of options and procedures.* Chicago: American Library Association.

McClure, C. R., J. Ryan, and W. E. Moen. 1993. The role of public libraries in the use of Internet/NREN information services. *Library and Information Science Research* 15:7–34.

McCrossen, A. 2006. "One more cathedral" or "mere lounging places for bummers"? The cultural politics of leisure and the public library in Gilded Age America. *Libraries and the Cultural Record* 41 (2): 169–188.

Minow, M. 1997. Filters and the public library: A legal and policy analysis. *First Monday* 2 (12). www.firstmonday.org/issues/issue2_12/minow/.

Morehead, J. 1999. *Introduction to United States government information sources.* Englewood, CO: Libraries Unlimited.

National Telecommunications and Information Administration. 2008. *Networked nation: Broadband in America 2007.* Washington DC: National Telecommunications and Information Administration.

Nelson, S. 2001. *The new planning for results: A streamlined approach.* Chicago: American Library Association.

———. 2008. *Strategic planning for results.* Chicago: American Library Association.

OCLC. 2007. *Sharing, privacy and trust in our networked world.* Dublin, OH: OCLC.

Peltz, R. J. 2002. Use "the filter you were born with": The unconstitutionality of mandatory Internet filtering for adult patrons of public libraries. *Washington Law Review* 77:397–479.

Pittman, R. 2001. Sex, democracy, and videotape. In *Libraries and democracy: The cornerstones of liberty,* ed. N. Kranich. Chicago: American Library Association.

Preer, J. L. 2006. "Louder please": Using historical research to foster professional identity in LIS students. *Libraries and the Cultural Record* 41:487–496.

Public Agenda. 2006. *Long overdue: A fresh look at public and leadership attitudes about libraries in the 21st century.* New York: Public Agenda.

Public Library Association. 2007. *Public library data service statistical report.* Chicago: American Library Association.

Putnam, R. D. 1999. *Bowling alone: The collapse and revival of American community*. New York: Simon and Schuster.

Rayward, W. B., and C. Jenkins. 2007. Libraries in times of war, revolution, and social change. *Library Trends* 55 (3): 361–369.

Reddick, T. M. 2004. Building and running a collaborative Internet filter is akin to a Kansas barn raising. *Computers in Libraries*, April, 10–14.

Reith, D. 1984. The library as social agency. In *The library in society*, ed. A. R. Rogers and K. McChesney, 5–16. Littleton, CO: Libraries Unlimited.

Robbin, L. S. 1996. *Censorship and the American library: The American Library Association's response to threats to intellectual freedom*. Westport, CT: Greenwood.

Rogers, R. A. 1984. An introduction to philosophies of librarianship. In *The library in society*, ed. A. R. Rogers and K. McChesney, 17–32. Littleton, CO: Libraries Unlimited.

Samek, T. 2001. *Intellectual freedom and social responsibility in American librarianship, 1967–1974*. Jefferson, NC: McFarland.

Scott, P., E. Richards, and B. Martin. 1990. Captives of controversy: The myth of the neutral social researcher in contemporary scientific controversies. *Science, Technology, and Human Values* 15:474–494.

Seymour, W. N., Jr. 1980. *The changing roles of public libraries*. Metuchen, NJ: Scarecrow Press.

Shera, J. H. 1964. Automation and the reference librarian. *Reference Quarterly* 3 (July): 3–7.

———. 1970. *The sociological foundations of librarianship*. New York: Asia Publishing House.

———. 1976. *Introduction to library science: Basic elements of library service*. Littleton, CO: Libraries Unlimited.

Shneiderman, B. 2008. Science 2.0. *Science* 319 (March 7): 1349–1350.

Shuman, B. A. 2001. *Issues for libraries and information science in the Internet age*. Englewood, CO: Libraries Unlimited.

Simon, M. 2002. Will the library survive the Internet? What patrons value in public libraries. *Public Libraries* 41 (March/April): 104–106.

Smith, E. 1995. Equal information access and the evolution of American democracy. *Journal of Educational Media and Library Sciences* 33 (2): 158–171.

Stephens, M. 2007. Web 2.0 and libraries, part 2: Trends and technologies. *Library Technology Reports* 43 (5): 10–14.

Stielow, F. 2001. Reconsidering "arsenals of a democratic culture": Balancing symbol and practice. In *Libraries and democracy: The cornerstones of liberty*, ed. N. Kranich, Chicago: American Library Association.

Strickland, L. S. 2003. Copyright's digital dilemma today: Fair use or unfair constraints? part 1: The battle over file sharing. *Bulletin of the American Society for Information Science and Technology*, October/November, 7–11.

———. 2004. Copyright's digital dilemma today: Fair use or unfair constraints? part 2: The DCMA, the TEACH Act, and e-copying restrictions. *Bulletin of the American Society for Information Science and Technology*, December/January, 18–23.

Tisdale, S. 1997. Silence, please: The public library as entertainment center. *Harper's Magazine*, March, 65–73.

Travis, H. 2006. Building universal digital libraries: An agenda for copyright reform. *Pepperdine Law Review* 33:761–833.

Van Slyck, A. A. 1995. *Free to all: Carnegie libraries and American culture, 1890–1920*. Chicago: University of Chicago Press.

Webster, F. 1995. *Theories of the information society*. London: Routledge.

Weingarten, R., N. Bolt, M. Bard, and J. Windhausen. 2007. *The American Library Association Office of Information Technology Policy public library connectivity project:*

Findings and recommendations. Washington, DC: American Library Association Office of Information Technology Policy.

Weiser, P. J. 2008. *A framework for national broadband policy: Report of the 2007 Aspen Institute Conferences on Telecommunications and Spectrum Policy.* Washington, DC: Aspen Institute.

Wiegand, W. A. 1976. *The politics of an emerging profession: The American Library Association, 1876–1917.* New York: Greenwood.

———. 1996. *Irrepressible reformer: A biography of Melvil Dewey.* Chicago: American Library Association.

Williamson, M. 2000. Social exclusion and the public library: A Habermasian insight. *Journal of Librarianship and Information Science* 32 (4): 178–186.

Xie, B., and Jaeger, P. T. Forthcoming. Designing public library computer training programs for older adults to promote technical skills and personal well-being. *Public Libraries.*

Acknowledgments

We thank the many colleagues and collaborators who have worked with us on various research projects related to the ideas and data in this book. First and foremost is our frequent collaborator and good friend John Carlo Bertot. Although John was unable to participate with us in this particular book, he has been a key researcher and leader in the study of technology in libraries. Our longtime collaborator on the Public Libraries and the Internet studies, John has worked extensively with us on research related to many issues discussed in this book and clearly informed our views.

On a wide range of related projects, we have also worked with many other individuals. A few of the main characters in these studies have been Gary Burnett, Larra Clark, Denise Davis, Kenneth R. Fleischmann, Lesley A. Langa, Joe Ryan, and John T. Snead. Jennifer Golbeck deserves special recognition for providing thoughtful feedback on the book itself. But, ultimately, we are grateful to everyone who has helped us develop the concepts of this text, whether they realized they were doing so at the time or even realize it now.

Much of our data have been collected through studies funded by granting agencies—the Bill and Melinda Gates Foundation, the American Library Association, the State Library of Florida, the National Commission on Libraries and Information Science, and the U.S. Institute for Museum and Library Services among others. Support from funding agencies such as these is vital to research about public libraries, and these funding agencies deserve the gratitude of the entire library community.

Index